Studying American Government

A Vade Mecum

Studying American Government
A Vade Mecum

Kenneth M. Holland
Memphis State University

D. C. Heath and Company
Lexington, Massachusetts   Toronto

Address editorial correspondence to

D. C. Heath and Company
125 Spring Street
Lexington, MA 02173

Copyright © 1992 by D. C. Heath and Company.

All rights reserved. No part of this publication may be reproduced or transmitted in any form or by any means, electronic or mechanical, including photocopy, recording, or any information storage or retrieval system, without permission in writing from the publisher.

Published simultaneously in Canada.

Printed in the United States of America.

International Standard Book Number: 0-669-28255-3.

10 9 8 7 6 5 4

Preface

During fourteen years of teaching American Government to first-year students, I have learned the importance of helping students improve their reading, writing, and research skills. The need to combine substantive instruction in the subject of American politics with practical tips on how to succeed in the course has become even more pressing with the adoption by many colleges and universities of open admissions policies and with ever-larger numbers of nontraditional students returning to higher education or coming for the first time. My involvement with the Writing Across the Curriculum movement over the past six years has taught me that reading, study, and writing strategies are best mastered in political science, history, chemistry, or psychology courses rather than in courses devoted entirely to "writing" or "study skills."

This book builds upon the D. C. Heath Writing Across the Curriculum Series and my former colleague Neil Stout's *Getting the Most out of Your U.S. History Course: The History Student's Vade Mecum*, also published by D. C. Heath. It incorporates the most recent scholarship in learning theory. My goal was to provide a practical guide to success in the Introduction to American Government course. Much of the material, however, is applicable to other political science courses. I wish to thank Paul Smith, Senior Acquisitions Editor in the College Division of D. C. Heath, for suggesting the need for such a guide and for his enthusiastic support during its completion.

Kenneth M. Holland

Acknowledgments

Author and publisher gratefully acknowledge the fine suggestions made by Ann C. Beck (New Mexico State University) and James L. Regens (The University of Georgia) in the course of the development of this guide. The author also extends his gratitude to the reference staff of Memphis State University's Brister Library, with special thanks to reference librarians Elizabeth H. Park and Norma Janell Rudolph.

Contents

1 Studying American Government **1**

2 Writing in American Government **43**

3 Using the Library and Documenting Sources **59**

Appendix: Careers in Political Science **95**

References **99**

1

Studying American Government

What Is Political Science?
Types of Politics

Take a stool in a local diner or the window seat on the flight from Chicago to Denver and listen to the conversations buzzing about you. More likely than not the air will be filled with talk of politics. Pick up a morning newspaper or turn on the radio or television at six o'clock and you will learn that "the news" consists largely of what is new in politics. Americans are fascinated with the virtues and vices of their governmental leaders and the successes and failings, the justice and injustice, of existing and proposed public policies. As a college student, you will feel continuously the excitement and tension politics generates as groups of students and faculty organize to advocate or oppose solutions to a variety of public problems. Campuses are scenes of colorful posters, painted slogans, noisy demonstrations, and impassioned debates concerning issues of local, state, federal, and international politics.

Political science courses are different from courses in physics, mathematics, psychology, or even history, because politics is a subject on which almost everyone has an opinion. Opinion, however, is not the same as knowledge. The most persuasive arguments are the most informed. Political scientists provide the factual background and the theoretical perspective we need in order to become more effective advocates. The study of government, however, is not merely an applied discipline. The science of politics, like all sciences, seeks the truth regarding its subject matter, regardless of its practical implications.

Political science, in fact, is one of the oldest of the sciences. Its founder is Socrates, a philosopher of ancient Greece, who, although initially interested in the natural sciences, such as zoology and astronomy, devoted most of his life to the study of human things. According to Socrates the most important question that a human being can pose is "How ought I to live?" The answer to this query, he said, is inseparable from the broader question, "How ought we as a community to live?" The fruits of the systematic study of politics have been especially useful to founders and rulers of nations. In a democracy, however, the rulers and the ruled are identical—"government of the people, by the people, and for the people," in Abraham Lincoln's immortal characterization. In order for popular self-government to succeed, each citizen must develop informed opinions on a wide variety of public issues, ranging from abortion to foreign aid, and become familiar with the workings of local, regional, and national government.

The political science curriculum is designed to assist in this process of civic education, to facilitate the analysis of political phenomena, and to prepare students for careers in which a knowledge of politics is considered necessary or desirable. The course that this handbook is designed to help you with the most is the political science course that more students take than any other. A number of states even designate American Government as a college graduation requirement.

If you wish to pursue additional coursework in political science, you should know that many students find courses in Comparative Politics and International Relations as natural complements to their study of American politics. An important component of politics in the United States is foreign policy. Political science departments offer courses not only in the relations between the United States and foreign nations but also in the relations between and among foreign countries, in international organizations such as the United Nations, and in the domestic politics of other countries.

Approaches to the Study of Politics

Political scientists approach the study of politics in different ways. Knowing something about these various approaches will help you understand the particular slant taken by your textbook and instructor to the fundamental material of American government.

Political Philosophy

Some researchers, in the tradition of Socrates, ask such questions as "How ought leaders to act?" "Which type of political system is best?" "Is war ever justified?" These "ought," or normative, questions are the province of political philosophy, a subject taught in both political science and philosophy departments. The theoretical approach is quite similar to the way most people think and speak about politics. For most citizens, seeking the right answer to controversial issues is the soul of the political life. Those political conversations we overhear are often arguments over the merits of a particular policy or system, such as abortion, gun control, deficit spending, socialism. Those political scientists who adopt the philosophical approach seek answers to these and the fundamental questions underlying them, such as "What is justice?"

Political Behavior

Another approach eschews, or avoids, philosophy and seeks to describe, explain, and predict political behavior. Political behavioralists adopt the stance of moral neutrality and utilize the scientific method of observation, hypothesis formulation, and hypothesis testing. They are neutral because they take no position on the justice or injustice—the goodness or badness—of political action. They ask such questions about American politics as "Which personal attribute of a member of Congress has the strongest power to predict votes on defense appropriation bills?" "How much influence does presidential campaigning have on midterm elections to the Senate?" "How tolerant are Americans on civil liberties issues?" Behavioralists attempt to account for and predict not only congressional roll call votes but presidential elections and Supreme Court decisions. To do this they rely upon quantitative methodology and the laws of statistical probability. Many of these quantitatively oriented political scientists devote themselves to the analysis of citizens' voting patterns or the measurement of public opinion.

Public Policy evaluate policies Pro/Cons to

A growing number of political scientists regard both the theoretical and behavioral approaches as too abstract or too academic. They want to be useful to the political community in a direct way. They serve the public by advising policymakers on the optimal solutions to nagging social problems. These public policy experts staff think tanks as well as universities and employ quantitative methods and systematic thought to evaluate existing and proposed policies. Policy experts pose such questions as "What is the most cost-effective strategy for reducing the highway fatality rate?" "Will abolishing the death penalty increase the homicide rate?" "What are the successes and limits of airline deregulation?"

How to Study and Think About American Government
Course Objectives

Your first exposure to political science as a discipline will probably be a course in American government. Whether it is required or elective, the course likely will have the following objectives:

- *To enhance your knowledge of the constitutional principles of the American polity and the workings of the principal formal and informal institutions of government—Congress, the presidency, the bureaucracy, the judiciary, political parties, and interest groups.* Some textbooks contain additional material on the various fields of public policy, such as economic, welfare, and foreign policy, and on state and local government. In general, your instructor will help you understand how government in the United States is supposed to work and how it actually works. You will be expected to be able to explain how and why particular policies emerge from the major political institutions. Why, for instance, since 1968 have Republicans found it relatively easy to win presidential elections but overwhelmingly difficult to gain a majority of the seats in the House and Senate? Why do most agreements between the United States and foreign nations take the form of executive agreements rather than treaties?

- *To develop your skills as a citizen.* Your instructor may not be content with introducing you to the "nuts and bolts" of American government and thus may also try to achieve the objective of imparting to you the skills and knowledge associated with effective citizenship. This civic education may take the form of instruction in the duties of citizenship, such as obeying the law, registering to vote, and serving on juries; or in the rights of citizens, including First Amendment rights to speak, write, or demonstrate in order to protest injustice and seek redress of grievances. Your American politics course may also be designed to heighten your sensitivity to matters of race, class, and gender and increase your tolerance for cultures different from your own.

- *To improve your ability to read actively and to think critically.* One of the shocks that first-year students often experience is the realization that college courses are nothing like those in high school. Your instructor is likely to demand that you do a great deal more reading, thinking, and writing than you are accustomed to. The level of the material and the instruction will be measurably higher and will take for granted that you have reached an advanced level of intellectual development. Keep in mind that fewer than half of high school graduates will attend a two- or four-year college. In the United States, secondary education is made available to everyone and its universality is supported by state compulsory attendance laws, whereas higher education is available only to those willing and able to accept its challenges.

Your Peers

Will your fellow students be like you, and how many of them can you expect in your American government class?

Student Background

The great majority of students who enroll in an American government course have never studied political science before. High schools typically offer American history, social studies, and even civics, but not political science per se. American government is usually the first introduction to the discipline and is taken in the first or second year as a required course. Experience indicates that "draftees" do as well as "volunteers" in the course and are just as likely eventually to become political science majors. The typical college student changes majors three times. So don't be surprised if during the term you begin thinking of swapping your biology for a political science major.

Class Size

How many fellow students can you expect in the American government classroom? Size will vary from approximately twenty to a thousand. At large public universities with doctoral programs in political science, the standard practice is for a professor, who may be quite distinguished in the discipline, to lecture to a class of several hundred twice a week, and for the students in groups of twenty or so to meet once a week with a graduate student in small break-out sessions. These are often called "discussion sections," because their purpose is to provide an opportunity to discuss the reading assignments and lectures for that week. The graduate students, who are either M.A. or Ph.D. candidates, are often not much older than the undergraduates, but they have completed a number of political science courses and have done considerable research. Increasingly, these graduate "teaching assistants" have received formal training in how to teach undergraduates.

It is important to understand that the graduate student who leads your discussion section may also grade your tests, examinations, and other written work. You will want to inquire whether this is the case. Look upon the break-out sessions as an opportunity both to impress the teaching assistant with your interest and knowledge in American politics and to clarify points or terms raised in the lectures or readings. It is imperative that you attend all discussion sessions as well as lectures. Review class notes and come prepared to ask the teaching assistant specific questions. In the large lecture theater, try to sit near the front, as close to the speaker as possible. You will be less distracted by those around you and more likely to become engaged in the material. In some universities, graduate students have full responsibility for the American government course and do all the lecturing. Where this is the case, class size is often in the thirty to sixty range. If you have a choice between sections taught by teaching assistants and others taught by regular faculty members, it is good advice to choose the latter. You will benefit from their higher level of training, experience, and scholarship. If the course schedule is unclear as to the status of the teacher, check the names against the university catalogue's list of faculty or inquire at the departmental office.

The following section outlines some practical tips for ensuring success in your American government course.

Reading and Studying Strategies
Managing Time

The key to success in an American government class is good study habits. To study effectively and efficiently requires that you manage your time. Time management consists of self-discipline, goal-setting, and scheduling (Nist and Diehl 1990, 33–44).

Self-Discipline

As a college student you can no longer rely on your parents to see that you attend class and study every day. You must supply the discipline needed to set goals and follow a daily plan to achieve them.

Goal Setting

The best means of developing sound study habits is to become goal-oriented. At the beginning of the term, as soon as you have obtained the syllabus and course readings, define your goals and make a plan to accomplish them. Taking a course is like charting a route on a highway map in order to arrive at your destination. If you know where you are headed, you can avoid destructive detours. By following these steps, you can assure yourself of success (Ziegler 1988):

1. *Identify your goal.* "To earn an *A* in my American government course."
2. *Describe why you wish to achieve this goal.* "I need a high grade point average to get into a good law school."
3. *Pick a date for achievement of the goal.* "May 9, the date of the final examination."
4. *List the things you must have or do to achieve the goal.* "Attend all lectures and class discussions, take good notes, schedule my study time, use the PROR reading and studying system [described below]."
5. *List the obstacles you must overcome to achieve your goal.* "I must resist the temptation to go downtown with my friends on weeknights." "I must kick the habit of cramming the material in the notes and readings into my mind the day before the exam."
6. *Divide your objective into daily tasks.* "Each day read five pages in my textbook and review three pages of lecture notes." Each daily task must be assigned a specific hour in which you will accomplish it. For this assignment, you will need a schedule.

Schedules

The first week of class draw up a general schedule for the remainder of the term. Block out on the schedule the time when your American government course meets. Use the assumption that you will spend three hours outside of class preparing for each hour spent in class. If your class meets three hours a week, you will block out nine hours for reading and reviewing. Thus, you might set aside 1 1/2 hours six days a week for studying, 7:00–8:30 PM, Monday through Friday, and 4:00–5:30 PM on Sunday. Also block out at least 15 minutes before and after each class meeting to review the reading assignment for that day and to review your lecture notes. Each week draw up a *weekly schedule*, in which you write down specifically what you will do during the time blocked out for American government. For example, on Monday, October 5, between 7:00 and 8:30, you will review Chapter 4 (15 minutes), read pp. 94–104 in Chapter 5 (30 minutes), and consult periodical indexes for a research paper on critical elections due October 17 (45 minutes). A good technique is to copy each day's schedule onto an index card, which you keep with you at all times, and place a check mark beside each task as you complete it.

Reading Your American Government Textbook

In an American government course, you may be asked to read several types of written work. Most instructors will assign a textbook in American government, which may or may not be supplemented by other readings. There are dozens of American government textbooks on the market, but as textbooks they all share some common features. A textbook is an author's presentation of the essential elements of a particular subject to a reader who is coming to that subject for the first time. The presentation typically takes the form of a summary of research conducted by other scholars. The textbook author has studied and digested the most important recent scholarship in the field and represented it in a readable form for college students. The strength of a textbook—its clarity and simplicity—may also be its greatest weakness. Textbooks, as a rule, do not challenge the reader's analytical and critical faculties. Nevertheless, mastery of the material presented in your American government textbook will give you a firm grounding in the subject, prepare you for advanced coursework, and assure you success in the course itself.

PROR: A Method for Effective Textbook Reading

The skills and habits that you developed for reading textbooks in high school will not be adequate in college. College textbooks present large numbers of terms, concepts, and relationships that may be complex and unfamiliar. To succeed students must develop a system of reading and studying that is both effective and efficient, given the limited time available to devote to any particular course. A system that incorporates the very latest research in learning is *PROR*, an acronym standing for **P**reread—**R**ead—**O**rganize—**R**eview (Nist and Diehl 1990). In our explanation of each of the four steps, we will draw examples from James Q. Wilson's *American Government: Institutions and Policies,* Fifth Edition (1992). The goal under PROR is to read in order to understand and to place what you understand in your long-term memory. To reach this objective requires that you read actively, not passively.

Planning to Achieve Goals

The syllabus says to read Chapter 2, "The Constitution," for Monday. It is now Wednesday. You consult your weekly schedule and see that you have blocked off 3 1/2 hours (1 1/2 hours on Wednesday evening and 2 hours on Sunday afternoon) for preparation for Monday's American Government class, in keeping with the ratio of about 3 hours of out-of-class preparation for each 1 hour of class. The first step is to make a plan to reach the goal of mastering the material in Chapter 2. Your allocation looks like this: Prereading (1/2 hour), Reading (1 1/2 hours), Organizing (1 hour), Reviewing (1/2 hour).

Prereading

The purposes of prereading are to generate interest in the material, to activate what you already know about the subject, to spark your desire to remember what you read, and to predict test questions.

Take an Overview of the Whole Book Preread the book before tackling the individual chapters. This involves reading the titles of the parts and chapters into which it is divided. American government texts are usually divided into parts, which in turn are divided into chapters. A typical textbook outline consists of the following parts:

- The Constitutional Framework of American Government.
- Informal Political Institutions.
- Formal Political Institutions.
- Public Policies.
- State and Local Government.

Note whether your particular textbook omits any of these divisions or contains additional parts. Each part consists of chapters. The section on informal institutions may include separate chapters on election campaigns, voting, political parties, interest groups, and the media. Chapters under the formal governing institutions will normally include the Congress, the Presidency, the Bureaucracy, and the Supreme Court. By becoming familiar with the chapter names, you can see how each lecture and reading assignment fits into the larger whole.

Note in the table of contents whether there are any appendixes, such as documents (for example, the text of the Declaration of Independence and the Constitution) or tables (for example, lists of all presidents and Supreme Court justices). Also note whether there is a glossary of terms, a bibliography or list of references, and an index. This end material can be invaluable in preparing for examinations and writing research papers.

To aid critical thinking, next read the book's Preface and Introduction. Most textbooks contain either a preface or an introduction or both, in which the author describes the book's main point, or thesis. Each part and chapter is intended to support this principal idea. The thesis provides unity to the different topics in the chapters. Knowing the thesis allows you to relate each individual fact and opinion encountered in the text to the whole of American national government. Political scientists do not agree on their assessment of either the theory or the practice of American politics. Thus, although the material covered in a dozen textbooks may be the same, it may be given a dozen different slants. It is the writer's thesis that provides the slant. The author of your textbook may try to prove the point that the framers of the federal Constitution have been so successful that the United States today is the most prosperous and free country on the globe and a model for numerous countries in the developing world. Another author may attempt to establish the irrationality and injustice of the American political system, which has resulted in extreme economic stratification, elite rule, and an imperialist foreign policy.

Preread Each Chapter Now you are ready to preread the individual chapters. Prereading consists of three tasks (Nist and Diehl 1990, 100–06):

1. *Read the title of the chapter and ask yourself what you already know about the subject.* In many of your courses, such as psychology, biology, and computer science, you will have relatively little background knowledge on which to draw. Although this is probably the first political science course you have taken, you will already know a great deal about the institutions and processes of American government, including political parties, the Presidency, and the Constitution. You will better remember what you read if you incorporate the information within your body of existing knowledge. In your notebook or journal, summarize what you already know about the Constitution.

2. *Read the headings and subheadings and ask what the chapter's organizational scheme is.* Chapter 2 contains eight headings, most of which have two or three subheadings. The basic structure seems to be chronological. The author traces the development of the Constitution from the Declaration of Independence in 1776, through the Articles of Confederation of 1781, to the Constitutional Convention of 1787, followed by the addition of a Bill of Rights in 1791, concluding with a discussion of modern views on the need for constitutional reform. The overall theme seems to be the emphasis the Constitution places on individual freedom (the word *liberty* appears in two headings and a sub-

heading). Ask yourself what you already know about freedom under the Constitution.

3. *Predict questions on key concepts.* The headings and subheadings contain several key terms, concepts, and events, such as Articles of Confederation, Shays's Rebellion, the Great Compromise, Antifederalists, and Separation of Powers. Write down some possible test questions: "What was the relationship between Shays's Rebellion and dissatisfaction with the Articles of Confederation?"; "Compare the Federalists and the Antifederalists."

Reading

As you read the chapter, keep two primary goals in mind: isolate the most important information and organize this information in a meaningful way (Nist and Diehl 1990, 116–24). Isolation requires identifying the key terms and concepts, distinguishing them from their supporting details, and selecting examples to illustrate them. Placing these concepts in your long-term memory requires that you recognize how they fit together. We can remember isolated facts for only one or two days; organized information we can retain for a year or more. A very powerful tool for isolating and organizing information is to mark, or annotate, your textbook.

Annotate the Chapter For most students, marking their textbook means to highlight. Highlighting, however, is a passive exercise that results in little or no learning. Throw away your highlighters and use instead a pen or pencil to write marginal notes. The habit of annotating will make you an active reader. When making marginal notes, keep in mind that the purpose of annotation is to facilitate review of the information before the test. Avoid underlining as well as highlighting, read and annotate one section at a time, and use your own words. Annotate the following items:

- definitions
- examples
- events, dates, and names

- lists
- cause-and-effect relationships
- comparisons

Figure 1 shows a passage from the Wilson text (31–2) accompanied by annotations in the left-hand margin.

Followers of Montesquieu thought U.S. should not have a national govt.

(criticism #1)
Liberty is safe only in small democracies.
↓
Madison's answer in Federalist papers:
(list:)
1. in small democracies, majority will be homogeneous and oppress the minority
2. in large republic, majority will be so diverse that minority will be safe
(EX:) weird people are safer in large cities than in small towns

(criticism #2)
Large countries cannot be real democracies.
↓
Madison's answer:
in large republics, the majority still rules, but safely
↓
the majority is a coalition of interest groups
(def:)
coalition = alliance
↓
the more groups in a coalition, the less tyrannical it is

James Madison gave his answer to these criticisms in *Federalist* papers 10 and 51 (reprinted in the Appendix). It was a bold answer, for it flew squarely in the face of widespread popular sentiment and much philosophical writing. Following the great French political philosopher Montesquieu, many Americans believed that liberty was safe only in small societies governed either by direct democracy or by large legislatures with small districts and frequent turnover among members.

Madison argued quite the opposite—that liberty is safest in *large* (or as he put it, "extended") republics. In a small community, he said, there will be relatively few differences in opinion or interest; people will tend to see the world in much the same way. If anyone dissents or pursues an individual interest, he or she will be confronted by a massive majority and will have few, if any, allies. But in a large republic there will be many opinions and interests; as a result it will be hard for a tyrannical majority to form or organize, and anyone with an unpopular view will find it easier to acquire allies. If Madison's argument seems strange or abstract, ask yourself the following question: If I have an unpopular opinion, an exotic lifestyle, or an unconventional interest, will I find greater security living in a small town or a big city?

By favoring a large republic, Madison was not trying to stifle democracy. Rather he was attempting to show how democratic government really works, and what can make it work better. To rule, different interests must come together and form a *coalition*—that is, an alliance. In *Federalist* 51, he was arguing that the coalitions that formed in a large republic would be more moderate than those that formed in a small one because the bigger the republic, the greater the variety of interests, and thus the more a coalition of the majority would have to accommodate a diversity of interests and opinions if it hoped to succeed.

Figure 1 Annotations

Note that the annotation includes **names** (Montesquieu and Madison), a **definition** (coalition), an **example** (strange people in big cities), a **list** (two arguments), a **cause-and-effect relationship** (smallness causes majority tyranny), and a **comparison** (between Madison's and Montesquieu's political theories). Also see that the annotations are in the reader's own words and that they are brief.

Organizing

If you simply read a chapter, within a day or two all will be forgotten. Therefore, regard the act of reading as only the beginning of the learning process. After reading and annotating the chapter, continue to put the information into your own words and to organize and further reduce the amount of information to be learned (Nist and Diehl 1990, 135–51). There are several study strategies that enable you both to organize key terms and concepts and to rehearse them repeatedly before the test. For the study of American government, four strategies are particularly useful: mapping, concept cards, charting, and time lines.

Mapping Mapping, or graphic organizing, is based on the premise that you will remember material better if you can see it. Maps show how ideas and terms are related. After reading and annotating the chapter, jot down a list of the key terms and concepts. Choose a single key term or concept and put that in the middle of the map. Beside it list its definition. Decide which broader class the term or concept belongs to and place that above the main term. Next, write any subcategories beneath the main term and any examples of the subcategories below them. List the definitions of each subcategory to the side, if necessary for clarity. Let's map a paragraph from Chapter 2 (24–5):

> When the convention decided to make the Virginia Plan its agenda, it had fundamentally altered the nature of its task. The business at hand was not to be the Articles and their defects, but rather how one should go about designing a true national government. The Virginia Plan called for a strong national union organized into

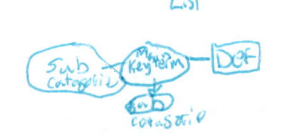

three governmental branches—the legislative, executive, and judicial. The legislature was to be composed of two houses, the first elected directly by the people and the second chosen by the first house from among people nominated by state legislatures. The executive was to be chosen by the national legislature, as were members of a national judiciary. The executive and some members of the judiciary were to constitute a "council of revision" that could veto acts of the legislature; that veto, in turn, could be overridden by the legislature.

The map in Figure 2 graphically presents the two essential features of the Virginia Plan and depicts one example of how strong the legislature was in Madison's proposal.

Concept Cards In high school you may have used flash cards to learn factual material, such as the vocabulary of a foreign language. The idea of a concept card is similar. Simply write the concept, term, event, or person on one side of an index card and its definition or description on the other side. On the front side, in the upper right-hand corner write a key term (to help organize the cards for study), the name of the person with whom the term is associated, and the number of the page on which the term is defined. On the back of the card, write the definition and an example. Figure 3 shows a card for a term introduced in Chapter 2.

Concept cards can be carried around for studying when you have a free five minutes. They can be divided into two groups—information you know and don't know—and cards with the same key term can be brought together to form answers to possible essay questions.

Charting Charting is useful when the instructor is likely to ask you to compare or contrast two items. *Compare* or *contrast* are common **command words** used in essay questions. List the items to be compared horizontally on the page and the categories in which they will be compared vertically. Figure 4 shows an example from "The Constitution" (24–5). Charting is quite useful in helping you reduce information.

Reading and Studying Strategies **17**

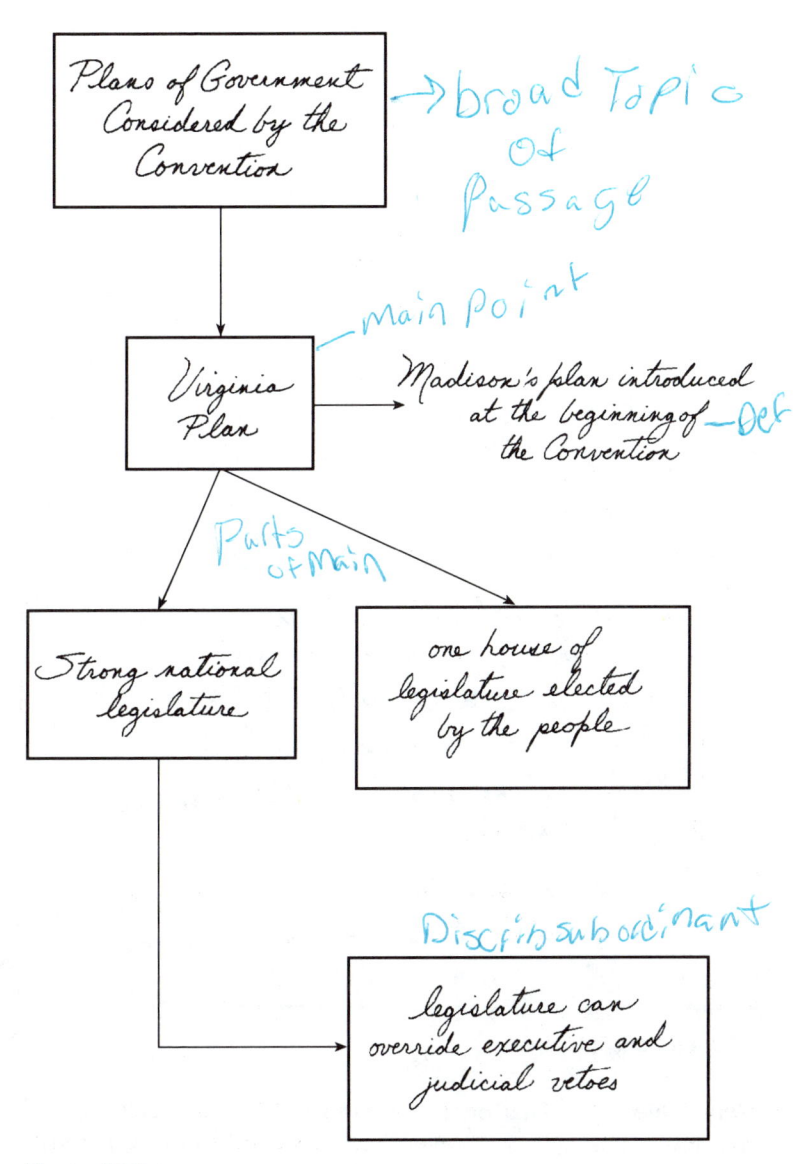

```
┌─────────────────────┐
│ Plans of Government │ → broad Topic
│ Considered by the   │    of
│ Convention          │    Passage
└──────────┬──────────┘
           │
           ▼                  main point
┌─────────────────┐     Madison's plan introduced
│  Virginia       │ →   at the beginning of — Def
│  Plan           │     the Convention
└────┬────────┬───┘
     │        │
  Parts
  of Main
     │        │
     ▼        ▼
┌──────────────┐  ┌──────────────────┐
│ Strong national│  │ one house of     │
│ legislature    │  │ legislature elected│
│                │  │ by the people    │
└───────┬────────┘  └──────────────────┘
        │
        │               Discrib subordinant
        │        ┌──────────────────┐
        └──────► │ legislature can  │
                 │ override executive and │
                 │ judicial vetoes  │
                 └──────────────────┘
```

Figure 2 Map

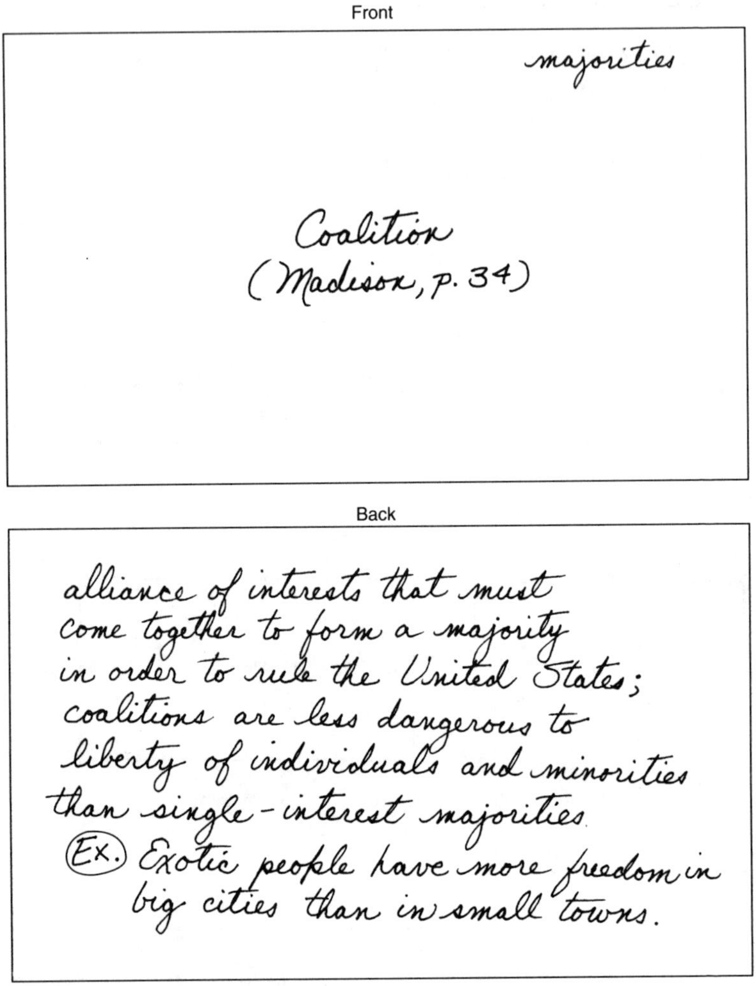

18 Chapter 1 Studying American Government

Front

> *majorities*
>
> Coalition
> (Madison, p. 34)

Back

> alliance of interests that must come together to form a majority in order to rule the United States; coalitions are less dangerous to liberty of individuals and minorities than single-interest majorities.
> (Ex.) Exotic people have more freedom in big cities than in small towns.

Figure 3 Concept Card

Time Lines The final organizing and rehearsing strategy is the time line. Time lines work well when you are studying chronological events. This is a technique you will want to employ often, because American government textbooks are full of historical

	Virginia Plan	New Jersey Plan
Attitude toward Articles of Confed.	Hostile	Friendly
Locus of Sovereignty	National government	The states
Apportionment of seats in Congress	By population	Each state has one vote regardless of how many representatives it sends
Mission of Congress	To represent the people	To represent the states

Figure 4 Chart

sequences. First choose the beginning and ending dates, then put the beginning date in the left-hand column and write the event that occurred on that date to the right. Continue down the paper, dates on the left, key events on the right. Figure 5 shows a time line for the period 1776–1791, a critical era in the nation's founding (Wilson 1992, 15–33).

Rehearsal You can use maps, concept cards, charts, and time lines to rehearse the key information you have selected from the

The Founding Period

1776   Declaration of Independence signed

1776   Eight states adopt written constitutions, including bills of rights and representative democracy

1781   Articles of Confederation go into effect; league of sovereign states; Congress cannot raise taxes or regulate commerce; no national judicial system

1787   Constitutional Convention meets in Philadephia; ignores its congressional mandate and adopts a plan to establish a national government.

1787   Constitutional Convention meets in Philadephia; ignores its congressional mandate and adopts a plan to establish a national government.

1788   Constitution ratified by a sufficient number of states

1791   Bill of Rights goes into effect; promised by supporters of the Constitution during ratification debates

Figure 5 Time Line

Declaration of Independence
Articles of Confederation
State Constitutions
Shays's Rebellion
Constitutional Convention
Virginia Plan
Great Compromise
Montesquieu v. Madison
Slavery
Framer's Motives
<u>Federalist Papers</u>
Antifederalists
Amending
Bill of Rights
Modern criticisms of the Constitution

Figure 6 Note Card for Reviewing

6. Does the argument suffer from any logical fallacies? (See below.)

A fallacy is an error in reasoning that has the appearance of soundness. Some of the most common ones are as follows:

- *"after this, therefore because of this."* Here something is assumed to be the cause of something else merely because it preceded it in time. *Example:* "Jimmy Carter lost the 1980 presidential election because in 1979 Iranian revolutionaries took hostage the Americans working at the U.S. embassy in Teheran." President Carter's failure to win the hostages' release certainly contributed to his defeat, but there were many other ingredients in Ronald Reagan's 1980 victory. There is every indication that Reagan would have won even in the absence of a hostage crisis.

- *"against the person."* The writer attacks the individual making the argument rather than the argument itself. *Example:* "Senator Smith's opposition to gun control is unconvincing." "But how do you know?" "The Senator had only a *C* average in law school." Senator Smith may indeed possess only average intelligence but his argument on this issue may still be stronger than that of his opponents. Arguments can stand by themselves.

- *"begging the question."* This is an attempt to demonstrate a conclusion by means of premises that themselves need to be demonstrated. *Example:* "Mary Ann always votes wisely." "But how do you know?" "Because she always votes Republican." This answer assumes that Republicans make better public servants than Democrats. The speaker has not proven this conclusion, however.

- *"hasty generalization."* In this case, the writer argues improperly from a special case to a general rule. *Example:* "Marxism is a system based on false beliefs." "But how do you know?" "Because it failed in the Soviet Union." Although the Soviet Union's economy is in shambles, that is not necessarily an indictment of Karl Marx's teachings. The Chinese claim that Moscow abandoned Marxism long ago and that it works where it is seriously tried.

- *"it does not follow."* This error occurs when there is lack of connection between the premise and the conclusion drawn from it. *Example:* "A country that can put a man on the moon can certainly solve the homelessness problem." Winning the race to the moon, a national mission announced by President John F. Kennedy, required very different kinds of resources and policies than eliminating homelessness does. The speaker is comparing apples and oranges. You cannot infer capacity to solve one problem from success at fulfilling a very different kind of mission.

Summary, Analysis, Synthesis

As you can tell from the six questions listed in the previous section, critical thinking is the product of summary, analysis, and synthesis. To illustrate, let's take another passage from Wilson's *American Government:*

> Client-serving programs led to the creation of client-serving government agencies. Some scholars have spoken of such agencies as the Civil Aeronautics Board or the Federal Communications Commission as having been "captured" by the groups that they were supposed to regulate, but this is a misreading of history. These agencies and others like them were formed specifically to serve the interests of domestic aviation and radio broadcasting, just as the Veterans Administration was created to serve the interests of veterans. At the time that these laws were passed and for many years thereafter, people saw nothing wrong with such promotional ventures.
>
> Important political changes have substantially reduced the freedom of action of client-serving agencies. The greater ease with which one can form and sustain groups purporting to represent mass or diffuse interests and the larger range of questions in which federal courts now intervene have made low-visibility client politics less common than in the past. Even tobacco farmers have had to accept lesser subsidies because of popular concerns over smoking. Naderite groups, environmental-protection groups, and organizations representing liberal and conservative causes use sophisticated fund-raising methods and take advantage of the

easier access that plaintiffs have to courts (owing to changed rules on standing and provisions for fee shifting). By these methods such groups have reduced the extent to which diffuse interests go unrepresented in the arena of client politics but have created new problems because that representation is often inaccurate. (1992, 616)

Summary

There are a number of facts in these two paragraphs, among them that Congress established the Federal Communications Commission (FCC) to serve the interests of radio broadcasting and reduced the subsidies for tobacco farmers because of changes in public opinion concerning smoking. Memorizing these facts, however, will not help you understand the meaning of the passage. These are only examples backing the thesis of these paragraphs. But what is the thesis? First, let's try to **summarize** what we have just read:

> Some scholars believe that federal administrative agencies act counter to the public interest because they are controlled by the sector of the economy they were intended to regulate. This view is inaccurate, however, because groups claiming to represent the public interest use sophisticated fund-raising methods and easy access to the courts to reduce agencies' freedom of action.

Summarizing forced us to discover the author's main point, that the so-called "iron triangle theory" of agency–interest-group–congressional committee relations cannot explain the behavior of many federal agencies, including the FCC and the Department of Agriculture.

Analysis

Now, let's try **analysis**. Wilson points out that scholars have made two errors in characterizing agency behavior. First, they have claimed that Congress intended agencies such as the Civil Aeronautics Board (CAB) and the FCC to promote the public interest, when in fact their legislative mandate was to promote the welfare of commercial aviation and radio broadcasting. Second, they have failed to take into account significant changes that have occurred since the 1960s in the agencies' political environment. Critics of agency policies, such as Ralph Nader, now can easily mobilize public opinion and the courts against regulations or subsidies that they believe do not promote the common good. In other words, these scholars have failed to take into account the impact of the public interest movement and judicial activism on client politics.

Synthesis

Finally, let's **synthesize** what we have learned in these two paragraphs with what we learned earlier. In Chapter 9 Wilson describes the emergence of Ralph Nader as a popular figure in the 1960s. Nader, a lawyer, formed various consumer-interest organizations that solicited thousands of small contributions from sympathetic individuals by means of direct mail. These organizations soon constituted an elaborate network pressing the claims of environmentalists, consumers, and citizens. Our two paragraphs, which appear in Chapter 23, document the significant effect the Nader network has had on the regulatory process. We also learn here that one of the most effective uses of the large sums of money raised from large numbers of small contributors has been the funding of lawsuits.

Reading Anthologies

Many instructors will supplement the American government textbook with a book of readings or a collection of essays and studies. Some will even assign an anthology in lieu of a textbook. This material will be more challenging, because it is original scholarship or journalism that has not yet been digested and analyzed by anyone. You will also find that editors of anthologies often intentionally choose selections with conflicting conclusions. To get the most from such a book, you should try to have the contributors engage each other in a debate—where a thesis confronts an antithesis. Your goal is a synthesis that combines the insights of each author with your own judgment. Editors of readings in American govern-

...dings according to the same pattern used ... Pro and con arguments on such issues as ...tional amendments, campaign reform, the Presi- ...vers, and gun control are presented. Note that many in... assign such readings for the purpose of stimulating discu... ...on, so be prepared to debate these issues in class. The better informed you are on both sides of the question, the more articulate and impressive you will be in the discussion. It is essential to read each selection using the PROR system and the techniques of critical thinking as outlined above, and with an open mind. After reading the essays on a particular controversy, jot down in your notebook, without looking back at the readings, a statement of the action proposed and a list of the major arguments for and against.

Reading Daily Newspapers

Some political scientists ask their students to subscribe to a national newspaper. The most common papers assigned in American government courses are the *New York Times,* the *Washington Post,* the *Los Angeles Times,* and the *Christian Science Monitor.* The publishers make these newspapers available for classroom use at a significant discount. Allocate one hour each day for reading the paper and follow these steps:

1. *Scan the sections on national and local news.* The front page belongs to the first, or "A," section of the paper, where you will find the news of national importance and the most significant news of regional interest. Most papers also feature a section on local news, which may be labeled "B," "C," "D," and so forth. Mark each story title that suggests a story with political content. News stories are supposed to be objective reports of an event. Decide whether this is true for each story you read.

2. *Scan the editorial and "op ed" pages.* Unlike reporters, editors are free to express their opinions, and their essays appear on a special page, called the editorial page. Opposite the editorial page, on the right-hand side, you will typically find opinion pieces written by local and nationally syndicated columnists,

such as Tom Wicker, George Will, David Broder, and Ellen Goodman, some of whom have reputations as political liberals and others as political conservatives. Can you tell who is conservative and who is liberal? Again, mark those items with political themes.

3. *Scan the letters to the editor.* Either on or near the op ed page, you will find letters to the newspaper's editor written by readers like yourself. These letters are often severely edited by the newspaper because of space limitations, but they can provide useful information and insight into matters of public importance. Mark those addressing political topics.

4. *Beginning with the front page, peruse each story, essay, and letter you have marked.* You need not read a news story entirely, because reporters are trained to provide the key elements in the first one or two paragraphs. Clip out those items that address matters of government operations, government officials (both elected and appointed), and significant domestic and foreign policy. Place them in an 8 1/2" × 11" looseleaf binder, organized to correspond with the sequence of chapters in your textbook or the course syllabus. Use this "clipping file" to update information in the textbook readings, as there is a one-year lag time between completion of a textbook and its publication. You can also use your file to help to prepare for quizzes and examinations and to aid in finding topics for and writing research papers.

Reading Primary Sources

There are two kinds of sources of information used by paper writers: primary and secondary. A primary source is a document or report of what someone has seen or discovered. Examples are the Declaration of Independence, Supreme Court opinions, letters, philosophical treatises, or articles published in scholarly journals reporting experimental findings. Secondary sources are summaries, analyses, or syntheses of primary sources. All textbooks and most books and articles written by political scientists fall into the category of secondary-source materials. Primary materials are considered more reliable than secondary interpretations, because scholars can easily distort the historical record, even without intending to do so. By reading documents and letters written by political leaders, you can get close to significant political events and reach your own conclusions regarding their meaning. Common primary sources assigned in the introductory American government course include the Declaration of Independence, the Constitution, and the *Federalist* Papers. Follow the instructions sketched above for reading critically.

Interpreting Graphs, Polls, and Pictures

Reading Graphs

Flip through the pages of your textbook or anthology. You will find (in addition to the text) graphs, tables, figures, charts, and maps. One of the best ways of presenting complex relationships among data is in graphic form. Graphs can convey certain kinds of information more quickly and forcefully than words alone. Depending on the numbers presented, graphs can either provide a snapshot of data for a single moment or show how a quantity changes over time. Newspapers and magazines, such as *USA Today* and *Newsweek,* as well as textbooks, are relying more and more on graphics to communicate to their readers. Graphics vary in complexity, however, and the meaning of those found in American government texts does not usually simply jump out at the reader. Experience shows, in fact, that most students skip over the figures and tables in their textbook rather than pausing to decipher them. To exploit the knowledge offered by your American government textbook and readings, examine each graphic and photograph and ask yourself how it illustrates or adds to the written material in the text. Refer to the **line graph** shown in Figure 7 as you review these hints on what to look for:

Interpreting Graphs, Polls, and Pictures **31**

———— House   ———— Senate

Mean percentage of first-term members

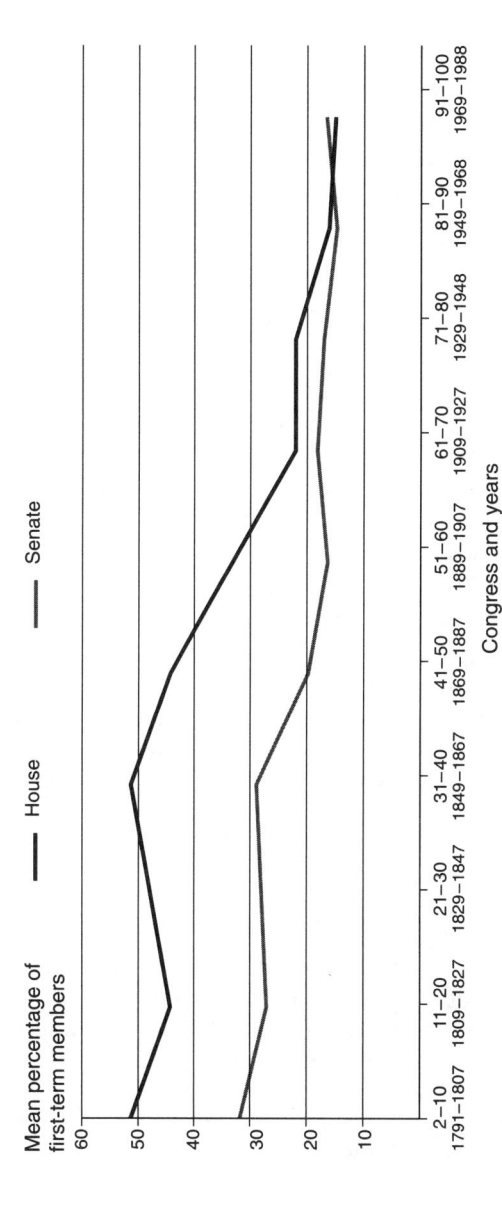

[Graph with y-axis 10–60, x-axis Congresses 2–10 (1791–1807) through 91–100 (1969–1988)]

Congress and years

Figure 7 Decline in Percentage of First-Term Members in Congress (Wilson 1992, 277)

SOURCES: Data for 90th through 100th Congresses are from *Congressional Quarterly Weekly Reports*. Data for 69th through 89th Congresses are adapted from Nelson W. Polsby, "The Institutionalization of the U.S. House of Representatives," *American Political Science Review* (March 1968), 146. Data for 1st through 68th Congresses are from Stuart A. Rice, *Quantitative Methods in Politics* (New York: Knopf, 1928), 296–297, as reported in Polsby, 146. Data for Senate are from N. J. Ornstein, T. J. Mann, and M. J. Malbin, *Vital Statistics on Congress, 1989–1990* (Washington, DC: CQ Press, 1990), 56–57, 59–60.

32 Chapter 1 Studying American Government

1. *What is the graph's title?* The title of the graph shown in Figure 7 is "Decline in Percentage of First-Term Members in Congress."
2. *What do the numbers represent?* The numbers on the vertical y axis are the mean, or average, percentage of members of the House of Representatives and Senate who were there for the first time. The numbers along the horizontal x axis represent periods of 20 years. Above each period is the number of the Congresses that sat during that 20-year period. Each Congress lasts for two years. Thus, the 100th Congress, most of whose members were elected or reelected in November 1986, sat in 1987 and 1988.
3. *What point is the figure trying to make?* As time has progressed, the percentage of first-term members in the House of Representatives has dropped from a high of 51% in the 1849–1867 period to a level of 15% in the most recent period. The percentage of first-term Senators also fell, from a high of 31% in the 1791–1807 period to 16% in the 1969–1988 period.
4. *What is the significance of this point?* The Congress is no longer a body of citizen lawmakers for whom legislative service is a temporary interruption in their professions and occupations but is now a full-time job, and even a career, in its own right. Members of Congress, thus, may try to avoid controversial issues in order to keep their jobs, which depend on not alienating large numbers of voters.
5. *What is the source of the data presented?* These data are drawn from four sources: two books, a journal article, and *Congressional Quarterly Weekly Reports.*
6. *Which paragraph in the text does the figure amplify or illustrate?* On page 275, the author states, "In this century the rate of turnover has declined, and Congress has become a full-time career for its members. . . . (see Figure 11.1)."

The graph illustrated in Figure 8, called a **bar graph**, dramatically presents the explosion in the number of civil cases filed in

Interpreting Graphs, Polls, and Pictures **33**

the federal trial courts between 1961 and 1990. From the differing length of the bars, you can see how much larger the number of civil cases filed in 1990 was. The bars also enable the reader to grasp at a moment the especially large growth that has occurred in civil rights, prisoner petitions, and social security cases. The graph supports the point that over the past thirty years the federal courts have made special efforts to make themselves more accessible to the poor and racial minorities.

All civil cases — 1961: 58,293; 1990: 218,000

Civil rights — 296; 18,793

Prisoner petitions — 1,020; 42,630

Social Security — 537; 7,493

Number of cases in thousands

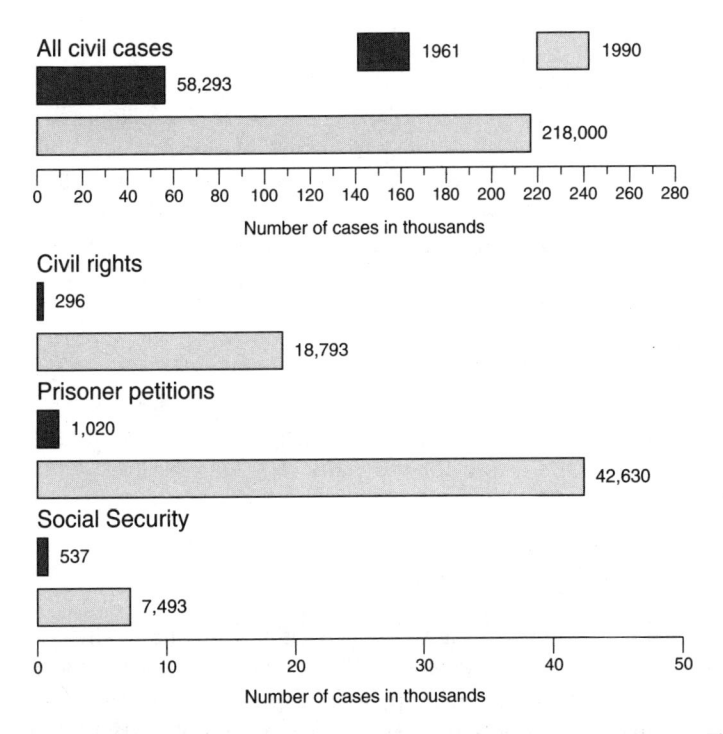

Figure 8 Civil Cases Filed in U.S. District Courts (Wilson 1992, 417)
SOURCES: *Annual Report of the Director of the Administrative Office of the United States Courts, 1975,* Table 17. Updated by author.

Pie charts are another kind of graph useful for showing quantitative relationships at one point in time. In Figure 9, for example, the "slices" of the four pies reveal the source of immigrants who have come to the United States since 1901. Note the dramatic shrinking of the European slice of the pie and the equally dramatic expansion of the Asian slice. The number of Asians moving to the United States now exceeds the number of Europeans. There has also been substantial growth in the percentage of the immigration pool from Mexico and Central America. The political consequences of these changes are manifold, including the enactment of nondiscrimination and affirmative action policies and changes in the curriculum of the public schools.

The extent to which a figure can simplify a complex mathematical relationship between two variables is illustrated by Figure 10. The vertical axis represents the percentage of the popular vote received by an incumbent president's party in a presidential election year, and the horizontal axis represents the percent change in per capita income in a presidential election year compared with the previous year. If you were to draw a straight line with half of the dots above and half below the line, it would slope upward from the left to the right, indicating that as per capita income rises the incumbent political party tends to win a bigger share of the vote. These data, then, support the hypothesis of retrospective voting, which claims that voters look at how things have gone in the recent past and then vote for the party that controls the White House if times have been good.

Reading Opinion Polls

Some of the data most frequently encountered in American government textbooks are the results of surveys of public opinion. Especially in the quadrennial presidential election years, your instructor may make frequent reference to current polls reported in daily newspapers and newscasts. Poll results are typically presented in graphic form and may appear somewhat daunting to the

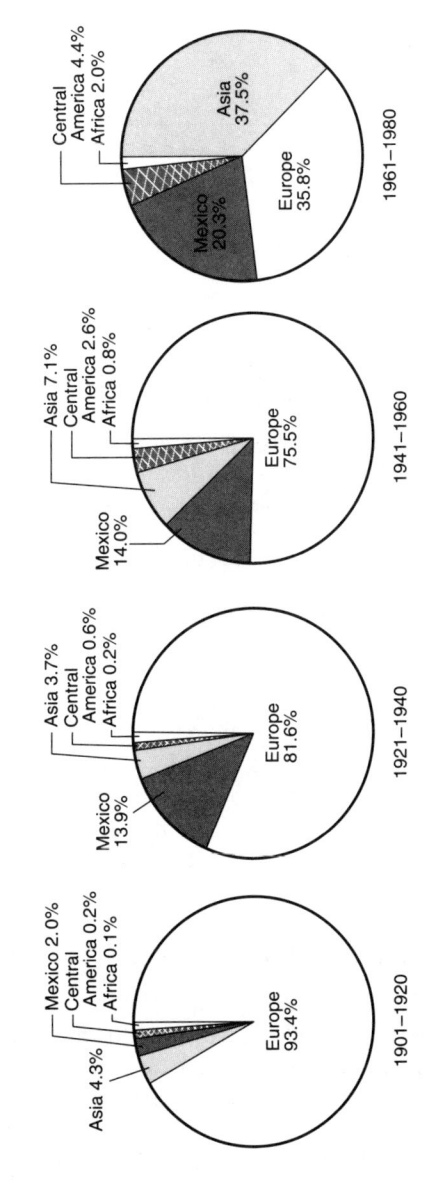

Figure 9 Changing Composition of U.S. Immigration, 1901–1980 (Wilson 1992, 499)
SOURCE: Associated Press. Adapted from a *Boston Globe* graphic by Steven Nelson. Reprinted courtesy of the *Boston Globe*.

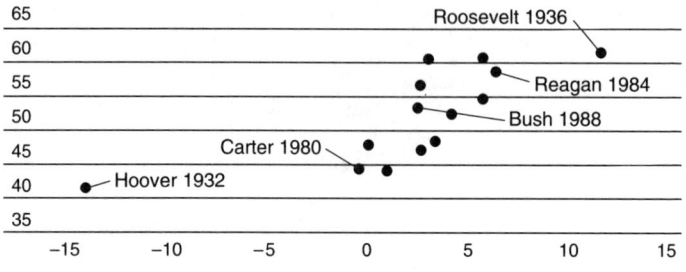

Percentage of two–party vote for incumbent party

[Scatter plot showing data points labeled:
- Hoover 1932 at approximately (−14, 40)
- Carter 1980 at approximately (0, 45)
- Roosevelt 1936 at approximately (10, 62)
- Reagan 1984 at approximately (6, 58)
- Bush 1988 at approximately (5, 53)]

Percent changes in real per capita disposable income in election year

Figure 10 Economic Performance and Vote for the Incumbent President's Party (Wilson 1992, 195)

SOURCES: Economic data from Thomas Ferguson and Joel Rogers, "The Myth of America's Turn to the Right," *Atlantic Monthly* (May 1986), 50. Election data from *CQ Guide to Elections,* 2d ed. Compiled by Professor John Zaller, Department of Political Science, UCLA.

NOTE: Each dot represents a presidential election showing the popular vote received by the incumbent president's party.

reader. These tables are actually easy to understand if you know the proper questions to pose. Table 1 shows a table typical of those found in American government textbooks. The pollster selected seven objects of public spending and asked a sample of citizens whether they think the government should spend more, spend less, or spend the same on each program. The respondents were then asked whether the government should raise taxes to pay for these programs. Refer to Table 1 as you read the following questions:

1. What is the population whose opinions are being determined? The table heading refers to "the average citizen," so we can assume that the group polled was a random sample of the adult population of the United States. The sample is random when each member of the population had an equal chance of being selected.

Table 1 People Want More for Less (Wilson 1992, 463)

The average citizen thinks that government spends too much. Most people don't want their taxes raised. But when asked about whether government should spend more, less, or about the same on various programs, the great majority favors spending the same or even more:

Program	Spend more	Spend same	Spend less
Medicare	74%	22%	3%
Social Security	63	31	5
Day care	57	34	8
Loans and grants for college students	46	39	14
Space program	32	44	23
The military	31	43	25
Food stamps	27	45	26

Taxes	Yes	No
Do you think the federal government should raise taxes to reduce the deficit?	26%	72%
Do you think the deficit can be reduced without raising personal income taxes?	56	37

SOURCE: ABC—*Washington Post* survey as reported in *National Journal* (April 18, 1987), 924, and (February 21, 1987), 444.

2. When was the survey done? The information below the table indicates that two polls were conducted, each in 1987.
3. Who conducted the poll? These two surveys were done by ABC-*Washington Post*.
4. What is the margin of error? Although not reported in Table 1, most polls have an error margin of between ±5% and ±1%. When the results are close, these margins can make a significant difference in interpretation of the survey.

5. What was the purpose of the poll? Why would a researcher want to know whether Americans think government spends too little or too much on the space program? The object here was to determine how much public support there is for reducing the federal deficit in order to allow us to predict how members of Congress will vote on spending and taxation issues. The results show very little support for raising taxes accompanied by strong demand that the government spend the same or more on most federal programs. We are thus not surprised if Congress continues to run a large budget deficit. Polls like this one illustrate the use of quantitative methods to explain or predict political behavior.

6. Which paragraph in the text does the poll amplify or illustrate? On page 462, we find a paragraph that concludes "see Table 16.1."

Reading Pictures

Photographs are both sources of information and useful aids in remembering key points in the text. Table 2 and the accompanying photograph together illustrate the point that the majority of children identify with their parents' political party. The author could have written a lengthy passage about Democratic, Republican, and Independent parents and their children, but note how much more economically and memorably the point was made by the table and accompanying picture. Notice that only 7% of Democratic parents have a Republican child and only 13% of Republicans have Democratic offspring. The data also hint at a weakening of party affiliation in the young generation. Approximately one-third of the children of parents who identify with one of the two major parties classify themselves as Independents. Each time you see a photograph, pause and ask yourself what point in the text or graphics the picture is illustrating. This is an exercise in synthesis. Stopping and inquiring will help you considerably in associating that point with a hard-to-forget visual image.

Table 2 Percentage of Parent and Child Agreement in Party Identification (Wilson 1992, 99)

	Parents		
Child	Democrat	Independent	Republican
Democrat	66%	29%	13%
Independent	27	53	36
Republican	7	17	51
(Number of cases)	(914)	(442)	(495)

SOURCE: M. Kent Jennings and Richard G. Niemi, *The Political Character of Adolescence: The Influence of Families and Schools* (Princeton, N.J.: Princeton University Press, 1974), 41. Copyright © 1974 by Princeton University Press. Reprinted by permission.

Young children displaying the party affiliations of their parents. (Wilson 1992, 100)

Reading Maps

Politics is concerned with place as well as time. All American government textbooks contain maps. Maps are used to illustrate such matters as the ratification of the Constitution, regional changes in population, presidential election outcomes, and party control of state governorships. Figure 11 shows an unusual map of the country, in that the states are drawn completely out of scale. As the note indicates, they are drawn in proportion to the number of electoral votes possessed by each state. To become president, a candidate must win a majority of the total electoral vote of 538. The map indicates that wise nominees will focus their efforts on the populous states of the Northeast, Midwest, and South, and also on California. It also reveals that a candidate could win the election by carrying only twelve states. Pause at each map, read its title

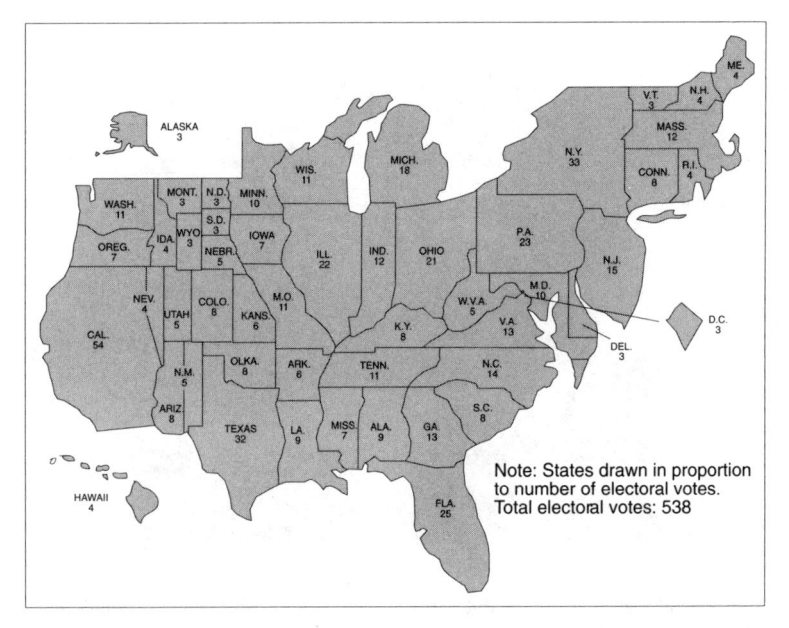

Figure 11 Electoral Votes per State for 1992 Election (Wilson 1992, 323)

and any notes, ask what you are supposed to get out of it, and find the portion of the text it illustrates.

Success in an American Government course requires not only efficient and effective reading and studying skills but also the ability to write clearly, coherently, and concisely. The quality of your writing will be an important determinant of your final grade. Chapter 2 provides some practical tips on how to improve your written communication skills.

2

Writing in American Government

At a minimum, in your American government course you will have to scribble lecture notes and take written tests. Many instructors will require more, perhaps a book review or even a research paper. This chapter provides some useful hints on how to get the most out of whatever writing is required and some suggestions for any writing you may want to do on your own.

Writing in Class
Taking Lecture Notes

Literally, a lecture is a "reading" by the speaker to an audience. Some lecturers read their prepared presentation word for word, others speak from a general outline, and some speak without aids of any kind. Some instructors make heavy use of audio-visual aids, including videotapes, films, computer monitors, slides, and transparencies. Some spend much of the period writing key terms and concepts on a chalkboard, and others simply talk. Some emphasize discussion and student-to-student exchanges; others expect the class to remain silent and attentive during the lecture. If the instructor's test questions are drawn, at least in part, from the lectures, then to succeed you must learn how to record a lecture for future study. Here are some tips on effective notetaking:

1. *Purchase an 8 1/2" × 11" spiral or looseleaf notebook, one for each course of study.* Do not combine notes from various courses in a single notebook. Strive for simplicity and flexibility. Looseleaf notebooks are preferable, because you can easily add

material, such as newspaper clippings and rehearsal strategies, to your notebook in the appropriate place.

2. *Write in pen rather than pencil.* Over time pencil script smudges and fades, rendering the notebook considerably less useful than it should be at examination time.

3. *Before going to class, read the material assigned for that day.* You will find it much easier to follow the instructor's presentation if you are familiar with the subject matter of the lecture. Spend fifteen minutes reviewing before class.

4. *Record main points.* Do not try to write down every word. Unless you have mastered shorthand or are taking notes on a laptop computer, you will not be able to capture every word. Effective notetaking is an exercise in discernment, separation of the verbal wheat from the chaff. Much of a lecture is devoted to illustrating and exemplifying the speaker's principal contentions, with a view to supporting the thesis. Keep in mind that the lecturer is working from an outline, either written or unwritten. Try to re-create this pattern in your notes.

5. *Write down unfamiliar terms.* Do not be caught on the final examination not knowing the meaning of a word mentioned in class by the instructor or appearing in your textbook. Make frequent use of dictionaries, encyclopedias, and other reference books to transform the unfamiliar into the familiar. Strange terminology is the easiest kind of ignorance to cure.

6. *Review your notes immediately after class.* Before leaving the classroom or within a few minutes of the closing bell, read over the notes while the lecture is still fresh in your mind. Correct any errors or omissions as you find them and then add a paragraph or two at the conclusion of that day's notes, summarizing the lecture and reflecting on the significance of the points made. This immediate review is an excellent device for facilitating retention of the material at test time. To make additions, corrections, and annotations of your class notes easy, draw extra-wide left margins (at least two inches) in your lecture notebook.

Taking Quizzes and Tests

The syllabus usually indicates the course requirements, including term papers and examinations. In addition to, or in lieu of, midterm and final examinations, some instructors administer unannounced, or "pop," quizzes on the reading assignment for that day. There is a variety of types of questions used in political science tests, including multiple-choice, true-false, fill-in-the-blank, matching, identification, short-answer, and essay. Find out from the syllabus or the instructor which type of questions will appear on each test, for each type requires a different kind of preparation. The key to preparing for nonessay questions is to identify and memorize the key points, terms, and names mentioned in the readings and lectures. Use the PROR system described in Chapter 1 to fix the key information in your long-term memory.

Writing Essays

Examinations in American government often demand responses in the form of expository essays. An expository essay is an explanation or description of a thing or process, as opposed to a narrative essay, which tells a story. To prepare for such a task you need to go beyond merely memorizing definitions and concepts. Here are some typical essay questions for an American government course, followed by the course objective it is designed to further:

1. *Compare and contrast* the mayor-council and council-manager forms of city government. (*Objective:* knowledge of local government)

2. *Analyze* James Madison's argument on behalf of a large, commercial republic. (*Objective:* knowledge of constitutional principles)

3. *Summarize* the principal arguments against the rule excluding from introduction at trial illegally seized evidence. (*Objective:* knowledge of civil liberties policy)

4. *Evaluate* the taxpayer revolt led by Howard Jarvis in the 1970s. (*Objective:* knowledge of economic policy and state government)
5. *Define* the iron triangle theory of agency behavior. (*Objective:* knowledge of how Congress and administrative agencies work)
6. *Explain* the functioning of the electoral college. (*Objective:* knowledge of the contrast between constitutional theory and political practice)
7. *Describe* the process by which a bill becomes a law. (*Objective:* knowledge of how Congress works)

As you can see, items on essay examinations typically begin with a **command word**, such as *explain* or *analyze*. Keep these words in mind as you read the assigned material and prepare for the examination. Use them as study guides. Another hint is to look for controversy in the course materials and master the arguments on both sides of a question.

When sitting for an examination, follow these steps in answering an essay question:

1. *Budget your time.* Include in your calculation the number of questions you must answer and the number of points assigned to each.
2. *Read each question twice, quickly the first time, and more slowly the second time.* Many students are penalized for giving incomplete answers or answers to a question that was not asked.
3. *Outline your answer.* On a sheet of scrap paper jot down your thesis and a list of the points you will make to support it. Review and revise your outline before beginning the essay. Follow the outline; do not try to tell the instructor everything you know about the topic.
4. *Write in complete sentences and coherent paragraphs, with a topic sentence in each paragraph and transition sentences connecting paragraphs.*
5. *Conclude the essay with a brief summary of what you set out to prove and how you proved it.*

6. *Edit and proofread your answers before turning them in*. Check to make sure you answered all parts of the question.

Keeping a Journal

More and more political science instructors have been influenced by the writing-across-the-curriculum movement, which stresses the role of writing in the learning process. Such instructors are likely to ask you to do a good deal of informal writing as supplementary to or in preparation for formal assignments, such as book reviews and research papers. One of the most common media for informal writing is the journal (Fulwiler 1987). Your teacher may ask you to write in your journal in class or out of class. Journal entries may be full of sentence fragments, misspellings, digressions, private references, and expressions of self-doubt. The entries read more like letters to a friend than polished academic prose. A journal is a place to experiment or to think on paper. Here is a sample journal entry made by a student, Laura, in an American government course. She has just read a section in her textbook entitled "The Effects of the Media on Politics" (Wilson 1992, 252–3), intended to help her understand how nongovernmental actors, such as the press and television, can influence the way Congress and the Presidency work. She records her reaction in this way.

I agree that tv commentary – what anchorpersons say about political leaders on the news, affects the popularity of presidents – and v.p.s. Sometimes I really feel sorry for Vice-President Quail (Quayle?). It seems that no matter what he does – or doesn't do –

he gets criticized on the news. I don't know if he is qualified to be president but at least Pres. Bush thinks so. It seems funny that in a democracy, where the people are supposed to make the decisions, tv newspersons should have so much power.

Note that Laura takes an idea from the textbook and applies it to her own experience. She is thus more likely to retain the information in the assigned passage than if she had simply read it through without pausing to put her reflections in writing. To derive the greatest possible benefit from your American government course, you may decide to keep a journal even if your instructor does not require one. Here are some suggestions for your journal:

1. Purchase a small looseleaf notebook (7" × 10").
2. Divide it into two sections: academic and personal. (The personal section is reserved for entries you do not wish to share with your instructor or other students.)
3. Record the date and time of each entry.
4. Write in your most comfortable style, the style you would use in a letter to a friend.
5. Write daily.
6. Write at least one full page each time, forcing yourself to "freewrite" when you can't think of anything to say. You can force ideas out by this technique.
7. Write a personal reaction to every assigned reading and to every lecture.
8. Include relevant clippings from newspapers and other sources.

9. At the end of the term, number each page and include a table of contents and introduction.

If you keep a journal you will find that the discipline of daily written reflection on your American government course is a powerful learning tool, and the habit of writing to yourself is a wondrous method of self-discovery.

Writing Outside Class
Writing Take-Home Essays

Some instructors, instead of examining you in the classroom during a scheduled block of time, will distribute a list of questions before the examination period and ask you to write essays at home and turn in the polished product. This is a very different kind of challenge than that presented by the in-class essay question. Frequently, you will be given a choice among a number of topics. Here are some tips on writing effective out-of-class essays:

1. If given a choice, select those topics with which you feel the most comfortable. Keep in mind that you are working with limited time.
2. Budget a specific number of hours for the preparation and writing of each essay. Allocate one-half of the time for researching the question and reserve the remaining half for writing.
3. Make a plan, marking on your calendar the day and time you will complete each essay.
4. Before beginning to draft the essay, state your thesis and make an outline.
5. Revise the first draft, that is, be willing to make changes in paragraph order and sequence of arguments.
6. Edit the second draft, correcting any errors in spelling, punctuation, diction, grammar, or syntax. If available, use a word processor, which greatly eases the revising and editing burden, including the spotting of misspellings.

The Writing Process

Suppose your instructor, in order to introduce you to a major public policy issue affecting the way the national legislature works, has asked you to write a 3,000-word essay on the issue of campaign reform. It is due in three weeks. How do you begin? Too often students founder at this point and postpone writing the paper until the day—or evening—before it is due. If you understand the writing process, however, you can avoid the procrastination trap and produce better writing with considerably less anxiety and stress. The most effective method of composition is the **process approach,** in which you work through three broad stages en route to your final goal: **prewriting, drafting,** and **revising.**

Prewriting

Prewriting encompasses all the preparations the writer makes before starting to draft. You begin by asking yourself a series of questions:

1. Do I understand the writing assignment?
2. Why am I writing this?
3. Who's going to read it?
4. What is this piece about?
5. Who am I as I write this?

Once you have established your purpose, audience, subject, and voice (serious or humorous, formal or informal), you are ready to propose a working thesis and begin to gather and organize information.

Drafting

After you have selected your topic, formulated a tentative thesis, and conducted research, you are ready to outline your paper. Never attempt to draft without first clearly identifying your main point and outlining the principal pieces of supporting evidence. The thesis you select at this stage may be quite different from the one you set forth at the project's commencement. (That is why it was called a working thesis.) The outline is only a rough plan, so you should feel free to modify it as the writing progresses. If you draft on a word processor, you will find it easy to make organizational changes, such as moving entire paragraphs or sections.

Revising

Most student-writers confuse revising with editing—reviewing a typescript for awkwardness in style and mechanical errors such as those in spelling and grammar. Revise comes from the Latin verb *revidere,* meaning "to see again." Revision means looking at a manuscript again with a willingness to make big changes. Professional writers often revise a draft five or six times before they are satisfied with it. The habit of drafting and then rewriting a paper at least once or twice is what separates exceptional from ordinary student writing. Before revising, let your draft sit overnight. This will ensure that your second look is a fresh one. If your instructor permits (and most do), give your paper to one or two others to read. Ask them where it is particularly strong and where they would like more information. Ask yourself how convincing your thesis is and whether you provided enough evidence to support it. A common error is for students to promise in the opening paragraph something that they never actually deliver in the paper. When you finally have a piece of work with which you are satisfied, edit and proofread it before submitting it to your instructor.

Writing Term Papers

Although more common in upper-level courses, such as The Presidency or Political Parties and Interest Groups, research papers are often assigned by teachers in introductory American government courses. Be sure to use the process approach described above. Plan the time available according to the following sequence:

1. Select a topic (if the instructor gives you an option). Begin by reviewing class notes and assigned readings. Examine your clippings file or journal. Is there a subject that particularly interests you? Avoid topics that are so broad that the research materials will overwhelm you, as well as overly narrow subjects on which little information is available.

2. Go to the library and utilize reference works and aids to locate relevant books and periodicals. (See Chapter 3, "Using the Library and Documenting Sources.")

3. Formulate a thesis and draw up an outline of the evidence you will offer in its support.

4. Unless otherwise instructed, organize your paper according to this structure:

   - *Introduction and Context.* Here you provide a statement of the topic and the background information the reader needs to appreciate the argument that follows.

   - *Thesis and Presentation of Evidence.* This is the longest portion of the research paper. Here you state your main point and supply the necessary supporting details and examples.

   - *Refutation of Competing Views.* Summarize those points of view that you rejected and point out their principal defects.

   - *Conclusion.* Restate your thesis and summarize the argument in its behalf.

5. Use a style manual, such as the one published by the American Political Science Association (described in Chapter 3), to prepare correct citations and references.

6. If permitted by your instructor, show the first draft to one or two friends or fellow students. Ask them to comment on parts they liked and on parts that could be improved.

7. Revise the first draft, being open to making significant changes and taking care to stay within the instructor's page limit.

8. Edit and proofread the second draft.

Avoiding Plagiarism

Plagiarism comes from the Latin word for "kidnapping" and means stealing and using the ideas or writings of another as one's own. Student writers too often commit this offense, sometimes unaware that they are doing so. The penalties for plagiarism can be severe, including a failing grade or dismissal from college. Irresponsible use of sources will cause the reader to cast doubt upon the value of your entire piece of work and will diminish your credibility. You assume the responsibility of representing an author's work accurately and fairly whenever you utilize the ideas, phrasing, graphics, or line of argument of another. Plagiarism is easy to avoid. All you need to do is credit the original writer for the borrowed words or ideas. Here are some simple rules to help you avoid using work that is not your own without giving appropriate credit:

1. When conducting research, do not copy word for word the work of others; summarize and paraphrase. It is easy for exact quotations to appear inadvertently in a student paper without the quotation marks because the researcher had forgotten that the notes were a verbatim report. Moreover, extensive quotation is a sign that you have not understood the subject on which you are writing or have nothing of your own to say.
2. Use a footnote or parenthetical citation whenever you include an exact quotation.
3. Attribute not only direct quotations but also paraphrases, summaries, organization of material, and lines of argument.
4. Be sure to give credit for any statistical information or graphics taken from any source.
5. Read more than one source on a particular topic and base your ideas on a digestion of the work of multiple authors. If the ideas are not those of any one author but represent your own synthesis, there is no need to give credit.

Remember that these rules apply equally to take-home exams and to term papers. Here are two examples of common forms of plagiarism:

Original

"Ultimately the only remedy for imbalances or inadequacies in interest-group representation is to devise and sustain a political system that gives all affected parties a reasonable chance to be heard on matters of public policy. That, of course, is exactly what the Founders thought that they were doing" (Wilson 1992, 237).

Plagiarism

The Founders of the United States thought that they had invented a political system in which all groups affected by a policy would have a chance to influence the government.

Although the writer has changed the wording, the essential idea is still Wilson's. As written, the statement appears to be the writer's own.

Original

"We suggest—based on the model of strategic behavior—that presidential campaigning will help [Senatorial] candidates. We also find support for this proposition. The positive impact of presidential campaigning is seen clearly in a series of mid-term elections, and sensitivity testing suggests that in many close races the president's intervention may mean the margin of victory. Last, we find that a presidential campaign appearance mobilizes voters, rather than converting them. In all, this soundly overturns the conventional wisdom, upsetting it on grounds of logic, theoretical development, and empirical support" (Cohen et al. 1991, 176).

Plagiarism

Presidents can help candidates for the Senate by actively campaigning for them in nonpresidential election years.

Because there is only one recent study that reaches this conclusion, the writer must acknowledge the article from which this information was drawn.

Writing Book Reviews

Instructors who wish their students to read beyond the textbook in order to gain a deeper appreciation of the theory and practice of American government may ask them to write a book review. This exercise exposes students to scholarly literature in the discipline and can help them develop analytical skills in reading, give them practice in presenting main ideas and supporting them with a line of reasoning, and encourage them to make critical assessments of what they read. A typical book review for an American government course will

- identify the book completely: author or editor, full title, publisher, and place and date of publication.
- describe the subject and scope of the book.
- give information about the author, focusing on his or her qualifications for writing the book.
- outline or summarize the thrust or argument of the book, giving the main pieces of evidence to support the author's position.
- indicate whether the author satisfactorily supports the thesis or argument.
- connect the book to the larger world by explaining the ramifications of the argument or material, by assessing the value of the book, or by placing it in the context of public issues or of other current books on the subject.
- relate the book's subject or thesis to a particular segment of the course.

Writing Letters to Newspaper Editors and Public Officials

Instructors sometimes seek to increase their students' capacities for effective citizenship by helping them improve their skills of oral and written communication. Citizens participate in politics in many ways other than voting. They read newspapers; watch television news programs and documentaries; join politically active associations; contribute money, time, and effort to political campaigns; discuss politics with others; telephone governmental bureaucrats with complaints; and write letters to newspaper editors and public officials. Even if your instructor does not require you to write such letters, you will find that your American government course equips you to do so. Writing public letters is an effective way of utilizing and reinforcing course material.

Although editors print only some of the correspondence they receive, if your letter is well written and thoughtful its chances of publication are good. Seventy-five to two hundred words is an appropriate length. Organize the letter carefully. It is actually a condensed argument and contains the following elements:

- Statement of the controversy or issue that you are addressing.
- Presentation of factual, noncontroversial, background information the reader needs to understand the issue.
- Statement of your position on the issue.
- Presentation of evidence and reasoning in support of your position.
- Refutation of opponents' arguments.
- Conclusion and call to the reader to take specific action.

More direct than a letter to the editor on an issue of political significance is to write to public officials themselves, those with the power to make the desired changes. You may wish to write to a mayor, city council member, agency head, legislator, governor, Senator, or even the President. There is evidence that policymakers, especially elected ones, pay heed to their mail and that letter writing can be an effective means of making government more accountable to the people. In this type of communication, your goal is to persuade the addressee to do or to forgo some action. Use the same sequence that you would use in writing a letter to a newspaper editor.

Writing and Critical Thinking

The more writing you do in your American government course, both in and out of class, the more opportunities you will have to hone your skills of inquiry and critical thinking. With its intrinsic fascination and controversial nature, politics is a particularly suitable ground for intellectual development. To fulfill this potential, however, you must go beyond the textbook and learn to gather, organize, and analyze information; make inferences from the information collected; test these inferences against reality; and use them to solve problems (Biddle and Clarke 1991). In other words, you cannot function at full capacity in the classroom unless you are an informed and efficient consumer of library services.

3

Using the Library and Documenting Sources

Learning to Use the Library

A college or university library is more than a warehouse for storing books. It is the very heart of the institution. Here is deposited the accumulated wisdom of the ages and the experimental findings and theories on which future scientific progress will be based. Here is where the undergraduate participates most fully in the community of scholars who inhabit an academic campus. Although one can observe politics at polling places and campaign rallies, the systematic study of government makes heavy use of the many resources and services offered by libraries. Academic libraries differ in significant ways from the public and high school libraries with which you are familiar. The reference department of a typical university library alone contains more than 40,000 volumes—more than the total collection of many public libraries.

In order to write one term paper, a student might have to do an on-line computer search of the library catalog, request guidance from a reference librarian, consult a dozen reference books, use three indexes on compact disc, seek assistance from the periodicals librarian to locate current and bound journals and newspapers, run four boxes of microfiche through a microform reader, request a computer assisted search of two databases, seek help from the government documents librarian in locating congressional hearings and Supreme Court decisions, read items within the province of the special collections librarian, and submit two requests for interlibrary loan. Many of these resources, especially those that are computer-based, may not even be available in your high school or public library. Thus, one of the best ways to prepare for your American government course is to take a guided tour of your college library, collecting handouts on all the services available to you and meeting the professional library staff on whom you will depend for so much and who will be happy to serve you. Becoming an informed consumer of library resources will not only make your effort to understand the theory and practice of federal, state, and local government more efficient but will also increase your power to influence political events.

How to Find a Topic

Suppose your syllabus says, "Write a 5,000-word research paper on some topic related to American politics." How do you begin? Do not go immediately to the reference librarian and ask for help. Start by reviewing class notes and assigned readings. Your American government textbook can be very useful at the beginning of a project. Is there a subject that particularly interests you? Are you more interested in how things are supposed to work or how they actually work and why, more intrigued by institutions or policies, more fascinated by government close to home or the government in Washington, D.C.? Phrase your interest in the form of a research topic or question to which you are seeking an answer. Avoid topics that are so broad that the research materials will overwhelm you, as well as overly narrow topics on which little information is available.

Too broad: "The Influence of the Rich on American Politics"

Although this is a very interesting subject, you will not be able to manage the mass of materials relating to class influence, and your treatment of it will be superficial and unimpressive to the reader. You try to narrow it but you go too far:

Too narrow: "Malcolm Forbes's Influence on the U.S. Senate"

The key difficulty here is the absence of a sufficient quantity of published material to permit any informed conclusions on the subject. Also, as topics become narrower they tend to lose reader appeal. Now you broaden it—this time successfully:

Good: "The Case for Public Funding of Congressional Campaigns"

On this topic, as you will discover when you begin to search the library's collections, there are documents (such as reports of congressional committees) and speeches, as well as a sufficient quantity of commentary and analysis on which to base a solid paper. Although perhaps not as appealing as the first topic, it is more manageable and still interesting enough to keep the reader's attention. You will want to predict how congressional behavior would change if members of that body no longer depended on contributions from political-action committees and individual donors.

When selecting a topic, keep in mind that you will want to reach a conclusion or judgment and cast it as your paper's thesis. Do not expect simply to summarize your research or describe your subject. To get from a topic to a thesis, use a four-stage approach, moving from your general topic to a specific issue to a research question to a working thesis (Lunsford and Connors 1989, 524).

General Topic	Congressional campaign funding
Specific Issue	Public versus private funding
Research Question	Would the benefits of replacing private financing of campaigns for seats in Congress with public funding outweigh its costs?
Working Thesis	Congress should enact a program of public financing of congressional campaigns.

An appropriate question to be addressed to all public policies, existing and proposed, is whether the costs exceed the benefits. Costs can be both monetary and intangible, such as infringement on freedom of expression. Expect to revise your thesis as your research progresses. You do not need to reach a firm conclusion until the research is complete and you have embarked upon the drafting and revising stages.

Search Cards, Bibliography Cards, and Note Cards

During your research you will need to keep on hand a stack of lined 4" × 6" index cards. On them you will keep a record of your search, the correct bibliographic information needed to document each source, and notes on the content of the materials read that will form the body of your paper.

Search Cards

Keep a record of the steps you take in the conduct of your search, noting on a search card each consultation of a finding aid, such as an index, abstract, or bibliography. This practice will prevent redoing work already done. Give your paper a short title and put it in the upper right-hand corner of each card. Place the name of the finding aid consulted in the upper left-hand corner, and list the particular volumes searched and the subject headings used. Each search card should look something like the one shown in Figure 1.

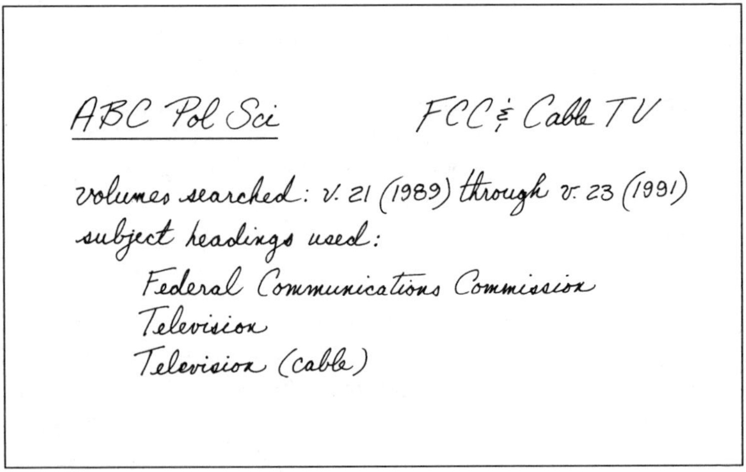

```
ABC Pol Sci                    FCC & Cable TV

volumes searched: v. 21 (1989) through v. 23 (1991)
subject headings used:
    Federal Communications Commission
    Television
    Television (cable)
```

Figure 1 Search Card

Bibliography Cards

As you locate relevant books, articles, and documents in the finding aids, prepare a bibliography card for each title. Each card must be complete in order to use interlibrary loan or to prepare the list of references you will place at the end of your paper. Use the reference format described later in this chapter. Identify the book's call number in the lower left corner, in case you need to retrieve it later. Figure 2 shows a bibliography card for a book, and Figure 3 shows one for an article.

Note Cards

In addition to search cards and bibliography cards, you will want to prepare note cards (see Figure 4).

In the upper right-hand corner of the card, identify the source by writing the author's last name. If you have continuation cards for the same source, number each one, as "1 of 3." In the upper left-hand corner, write the subtopic under which this information

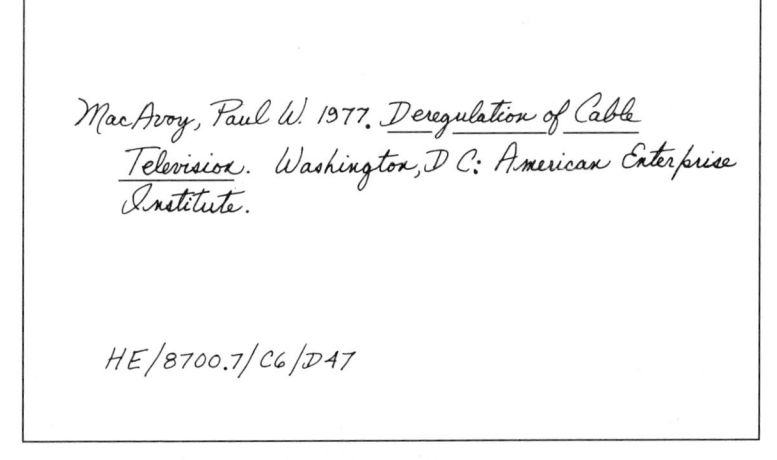

> MacAvoy, Paul W. 1977. *Deregulation of Cable Television*. Washington, D C: American Enterprise Institute.
>
> HE/8700.7/C6/D47

Figure 2 Bibliography Card for a Book

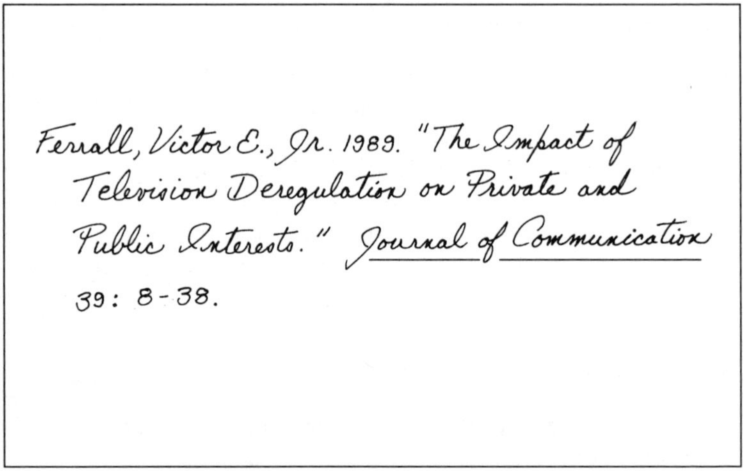

> Ferrall, Victor E., Jr. 1989. "The Impact of Television Deregulation on Private and Public Interests." *Journal of Communication* 39: 8-38.

Figure 3 Bibliography Card for an Article

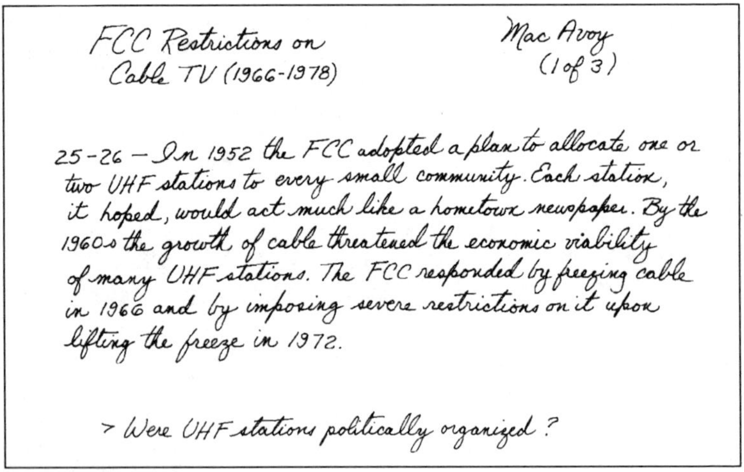

> FCC Restrictions on Cable TV (1966-1978)   Mac Avoy (1 of 3)
>
> 25-26 — In 1952 the FCC adopted a plan to allocate one or two UHF stations to every small community. Each station, it hoped, would act much like a hometown newspaper. By the 1960s the growth of cable threatened the economic viability of many UHF stations. The FCC responded by freezing cable in 1966 and by imposing severe restrictions on it upon lifting the freeze in 1972.
>
> > Were UHF stations politically organized?

Figure 4 Note Card

falls. Precede the note with the page number from which the information is drawn. Use the symbol ">" to set off your own ideas or questions. Before notetaking begins, you will need to formulate a working thesis and make a rough outline. The subtopic is drawn from this outline. Marking outline divisions on note cards makes it much easier to organize the information you have collected when you are ready to write the first draft (Rudolph and Argall 1990, 63–5).

On the note card you will summarize and paraphrase information gleaned from the books and articles you found relevant to your topic. Avoid simply copying quotations from your sources. Your goal is to read actively, not passively, and to develop your skills of discrimination and critical thought. Constantly follow the learning principles of "put it into your own words" and "consolidate and reduce information." Good research papers and essays contain few, if any, quotations. A quotation is a verbatim copy of the original; a paraphrase is a restatement of the original in your own words; a summary is a condensation of the original. Let's excerpt two passages from an American government textbook, dealing with the role of hearings in the process of making laws and congressional efforts to oversee the functioning of the executive branch. We will write first a paraphrase and then a summary.

Original

"Congress may compel a person to attend an investigation by issuing a subpoena; anyone who ignores the subpoena may be punished for contempt" (Wilson 1992, 385–6)

Paraphrase

Through its subpoena and contempt powers, Congress can force people, on threat of punishment, to testify in its investigations (Wilson 1992, 385–6).

Original

"Opponents of the legislative veto hope that future Congresses will have to pass laws that state much more clearly than before what an agency may or may not do. But it is just as likely that Congress will continue to pass laws stated in general terms and require that agencies implementing those laws report their plans to Congress so that it will have a chance to enact and send to the president a regular bill disapproving the proposed action. Or Congress may rely on informal (but scarcely weak) means of persuasion, including threats to reduce the appropriations of an agency that does not abide by congressional preferences" (Wilson 1992, 385).

Summary

The abolition of the legislative veto is not likely to change Congress's habit of passing general laws that give agencies a lot of discretion and then intervening when an agency makes a specific decision it does not like (Wilson 1992, 385).

Not only is summarizing the most economical approach to notetaking, but it is also the most useful to the writer. As you read the primary material and try to summarize it, you are forced to interact with it, to ask what the thesis and main points are. When reading sources, save time by condensing immediately after you have read a piece, while it is fresh in your understanding. For many of the materials you read, you will not need to make any entries on a note card because they will not address the precise issue you are researching. For every source summarized on a note card, however, there must be a bibliography card.

How to Use Reference Works

Your textbook and class notes may provide you with little or no information about your topic. Before you can utilize an index or library catalog, however, you will need to develop at least a passing knowledge of the persons, facts, events, and controversies relevant to the subject. This "first look" at the topic is thus very important. American government students find the following reference works to be good places to get an initial overview.

Encyclopedias and Dictionaries

Encyclopedias contain essays on topics; dictionaries offer definitions of terms. Three good encyclopedias for topics in American government are

Greene, Jack P., ed. 1984. *Encyclopedia of American Political History: Studies of the Principal Movements and Ideas.* 3 vol. New York: Scribner's.

Contains ninety articles, with an average length of ten pages per article. Useful for understanding constitutional principles and the evolution of political institutions, such as political parties.

Congressional Quarterly. 1988. *Congress A to Z: CQ's Ready Reference Encyclopedia.* Washington, DC: Congressional Quarterly.

Serves as an excellent source for the workings of Congress, legislative terminology, and biographical sketches.

Encyclopedia Americana. 1990. Danbury, CT: Grolier.

Is the best general encyclopedia for information on American public institutions and figures.

A particularly useful dictionary of both constitutional and institutional terminology is

Plano, Jack C., and Milton Greenberg. 1985. *The American Political Dictionary.* 7th ed. New York: Holt, Rinehart and Winston.

Biographical Dictionaries and Directories

In your reading you will often encounter references to people and organizations that are unfamiliar to you. An article about congressional campaign funding, for instance, might mention Jim Wright, the House Ethics Committee, or Common Cause, each unknown to you. A convenient way of learning more about such individuals and organizations is to consult one of the following works:

Who's Who in Government. 1972/73–. Chicago: Marquis Who's Who.

Provides information on officials in federal, state, local, and foreign governments. Is updated biennially.

Official Congressional Directory. 1982–. Washington, D.C.: Government Printing Office.

Contains a wide range of information about members of Congress, including addresses. Is useful if you wish to seek to influence political events by writing a letter to your representative or senator.

Almanac of American Politics. 1972–. Washington, DC: Barone and Co.

Profiles Senators, Representatives, and their congressional districts.

United States Government Manual. 1935–. Washington, DC: Government Printing Office.

Is published each year. Contains the address and telephone number for, as well as a description of, each department and agency in the federal government. Is useful for understanding the structure of the government, obtaining information on public issues and matters affecting you personally, and helping you to communicate your views to government decisionmakers.

Brownson, Charles B., and Anna L. Brownson, eds. 1987. *Federal Staff Directory: Containing in Convenient Arrangement, Accurate Information Concerning the Executive Branch of the U.S. Government.* Mount Vernon, VA: Congressional Staff Directory.

Lists top-level administrators within the executive branch, along with their titles, office addresses, and telephone numbers. Includes biographical sketches of 2400 key personnel.

Encyclopedia of Associations. 1956–. Detroit: Gale Research Co.

Describes almost 20,000 organizations and associations and provides their addresses. Is published every two years.

Guides to Reference Works in Political Science

If you do not know where to go to get a brief introduction to your subject, two very useful places to begin your research project are

Sheehy, Eugene P. 1986. *Guide to Reference Books.* 10th ed. Chicago: American Library Association.

Identifies and annotates the most important guides, bibliographies, dictionaries, encyclopedias, directories, handbooks, tables, biographies, and yearbooks in the discipline.

Walford's Guide to Reference Material. 1987. 4th ed. London: Library Association Publishing.

Covers most reference works in U.S. political science, including bibliographies, thesauri, encyclopedias, dictionaries, handbooks, and biographies.

Sources of Subject Headings

While you are having that initial look at your subject, make a list of subject headings. These are synonyms for your subject and specific subtopics included within your general topic. You will need these synonyms to make use of the aids described below, as articles and books are indexed according to subject headings. Without these headings you will be unable to locate books, articles, or documents. Your list should cover all aspects of your topic. State your subtopics in as many ways as possible, because all search aids do not employ the same subject headings. For instance, if in an effort to understand how foreign policy is made, you choose the topic of the role of the Senate in the formulation of treaties, you would find useful titles in periodical indexes, library catalogs, and bibliographies under the following headings:

Treaty-Making Power—United States
United States—Foreign Relations—Treaties
United States—Congress—Senate

The best source of library catalog subject headings is the following reference book:

U.S. Library of Congress. 1990. *Library of Congress Subject Headings.* 13th ed. Washington, DC: Library of Congress.

This work is supplemented quarterly with annual accumulations. It is a good place to begin your search for subject headings, because it will tell you what the library catalog calls your subject. You will also need a list of subject headings to conduct a computer search for sources. If your headings are too general, the computer printout will run several pages and list many titles not relevant to your paper. Precise headings are the key to successful use of computer searches.

Indexes, Abstracts, and Bibliographies

Equipped with a list of subject headings, you are now ready to use other aids for finding relevant articles and books. One of the best sources for research in American politics is articles in political science journals. They are more current than books and often contain information that may never appear in book form. To make use of these articles, however, one must first know how to find them.

Indexes The five best sources for locating relevant articles in American government are

ABC Pol Sci: Advanced Bibliography of Contents, Political Science and Government. 1969–. Santa Barbara, CA: ABC-Clio.

Comes out eight times a year. Contains law and court decision indexes as well as general political science subject and author indexes.

Combined Retrospective Index Set to Journals in Political Science, 1886–1974. 1977. Washington, DC: Carrollton Press.

Serves as a single index to articles published between 1886 and 1974, many of which were never previously indexed.

PAIS International. 1915–. New York: Public Affairs Information Service.

Appears weekly and indexes over 1,600 periodicals in the social sciences.

Social Sciences Index. 1974–. New York: Wilson.

Is published four times a year.

Social Sciences Citation Index. 1973–. Philadelphia: Institute for Scientific Information.

Is published three times a year. If you think you have located an important article that might be cited in subsequent research, consult the *Social Sciences Citation Index* for a list of recent articles citing that work.

General Periodicals Index The two types of magazines most useful in American politics courses are news magazines (such as *Time, Newsweek,* and *U.S. News & World Report*) and magazines of political opinion (such as the *New York Times Magazine, Commentary, Harper's, Atlantic Monthly,* the *New Republic,* and *National Review*). Most public opinion magazines speak from a particular political point of view—liberal or conservative. Articles in both categories are indexed in

Readers' Guide to Periodical Literature. 1905–. New York: Wilson.

Indexes articles from nearly 200 magazines and is especially useful for researching current political issues, especially controversies over public policy.

Abstracts Abstracts are often more useful than periodical indexes because they contain a summary of each article as well as its citation. You can discover by a quick reading of the abstract whether you need to go to the trouble of finding the article itself. American government scholars use six abstracts most frequently:

America: History and Life. 1964/65–. Santa Barbara, CA: ABC-Clio.

Contains brief descriptions of the contents of the articles listed.

International Political Science Abstracts. 1951–. Oxford: Basil Blackwell.

Contains abstracts from many U.S. journals, each about 200 words. Is published every two months.

Political Science Abstracts. 1967–. New York: Plenum.

Summarizes thousands of books, articles, and documents in each subfield of the discipline.

United States Political Science Documents (USPSD). 1975–. Pittsburgh, PA: University of Pittsburgh Press.

Part 1 is an index, and Part 2 abstracts the items cited in the index.

The American Electorate: A Historical Bibliography. 1984. Santa Barbara, CA: ABC-Clio.

Provides abstracts of almost 1,500 articles.

The American Presidency: A Historical Bibliography. 1984. Santa Barbara, CA: ABC-Clio.

Is another volume of abstracts in the same series.

Bibliographies You will want to find not only articles but also books on your topic. For this task a bibliography can be extremely useful. For books on American politics consult

International Bibliography of Political Science. 1953–. Chicago: Aldine.

Is issued annually. Covers books and articles published in American politics as well as other subfields of political science.

Books in Print. 1948–. New York: R. R. Bowker.

Use the excellent subject index for finding books on your topic.

Book Chapters Index Many books on American government are edited collections of essays written by several authors. For a particular topic, a chapter in one of these books might be the best source. Segments of books, however, are not usually listed in the library catalog or in periodical indexes. You can find them by using a special index:

Essay and General Literature Index. 1933–. New York: H. W. Wilson.

Is indexed by subject headings.

The Library Catalog Another means of identifying books about your topic is to consult your library's card catalog or computerized listing. You will also need to use the catalog to find books you have identified from bibliographies. Each book the library owns is listed here in three ways: by title, by author, and by subject. If you know the title or author of a book you want, simply find the book's entry, which shows the call number. The call number assigned to each book is unique—no other book in the collection has that number. That number tells you where to find the book on the shelves. A few libraries have closed stacks, denying students access to the shelves. In a closed-stack library, you fill out a call slip and present it to a librarian, who will get the book for you. If you are not looking for a specific book but want to see what is available on your topic, you need to search the catalog by subject. Of course, you will first have to identify relevant subject headings (see above). Some on-line library catalogs have keyword access as well as Library of Congress (LC) subject heading access. Keywords, like subject headings, can be general terms that include your specific topic, synonyms for your topic, or subtopics within your topic. If you wish to study the evolution of an important public policy affecting the health of several multimillion-dollar industries and the daily lives of millions of Americans, you might select the topic, "FCC Regulation of Cable TV." Start by trying these keywords:

General Term   Federal Communications Commission
Synonym   Television Regulation
Subtopic   Cable Television

If you went to the *Library of Congress Subject Headings* you would find this entry under "Cable television":

Cable television

UF   CATV
         Community antenna television
         Television, Cable
BT   Subscription television
         Television broadcasting

NT Satellite master antenna television—Access
UF Access to cable television—Law and legislation
BT Television—Law and legislation

UF means "used for" and precedes terms not used as subject headings. BT and NT are abbreviations for "broader term" and "narrower term," respectively. Headings preceded by a dash can be added to the main subject heading for more precise searches. If you tried to find "Federal Communications Commission" in the *LC Subject Headings* you would be disappointed, because the Library of Congress volume does not list proper names—of authors or institutions. However, if you used the heading "United States Federal Communications Commission" to search your card or on-line library catalog you would find a listing of books and other publications. For a complete listing of your library's holdings on the FCC, use this same heading not only in a subject search but also in title and author searches.

In order to do a comprehensive search, you should use both keywords and LC headings. Be sure to include the call number on your personal bibliography card for each book that might be valuable to your research. Many university libraries provide remote access to their catalog listing from personal computers or computer terminals located in other parts of the campus or off campus. Inquire if this kind of access is available.

The limitations of a library catalog are that it typically does not list individual chapters in books, articles in periodicals, microform items, or government documents and publications. You may need to consult special indexes for each of these four other sources.

Browsing You may browse the shelves, if your library has open stacks, and look for relevant volumes. Most university libraries use the Library of Congress system for classifying books. This scheme assigns the letter J to Political Science and K to Law. Finer classifications are made by adding additional letters or numbers, or both. The most useful general divisions for students of American government are

J 80–85 Presidents' messages and other executive documents
J 86–87 State documents

JK	United States
JS	Local government
KF	Federal law, including congressional hearings, reports, etc.
KFA–KFW	Law of individual states.

The Library of Congress Subject Heading volumes give more specific LC call numbers for browsing.

Library Databases

Published bibliographies are more complete than library catalogs, but catalogs are more up-to-date, so make it a practice to consult both. A resource that combines both the completeness of a bibliography and the up-to-dateness of a library catalog is a database, such as *OCLC, Prism,* or *Dialog.* If you punch in your subject heading or keywords, the screen will list all the books published on that topic catalogued by the Library of Congress, some of which your library may not have acquired but which you can get through interlibrary loan. Some libraries do not permit students direct access to these databases, so be sure to check with your library's policy. If student access is permitted, you may still need permission from your instructor, and you may be asked to pay for the search out of your own pocket. Before using a database you will want to prepare a search plan or, if not permitted direct access, you will have to fill out a search request. Some libraries also require a presearch interview, in which the librarian who will conduct the search will discuss your search request with you. Be prepared to provide both a narrative description of your topic and a list of subject terms:

- *Narrative Description.* Explain as you would to a friend what your search topic is, providing the background the listener needs to understand it, describing any cause-and-effect relationships, and explaining any specialized terminology.

- *Subject Terms.* List the subject headings and keywords you have identified from the indexes you have consulted.

Government Publications

Students of American government often overlook valuable sources of information and insight readily available in their library. One of the richest sources, especially for public policy topics or congressional and administrative behavior, is the frequently neglected government documents category. This category includes such diverse publications as the records of congressional debates and hearings, treaties, presidential messages, and studies commissioned by government agencies. State and local governments also produce informative documents. Three useful indexes to government publications and documents are

U.S. Superintendent of Documents. 1895–. *Monthly Catalog of United States Government Publications*. Washington, DC: Government Printing Office.

Catalogs all federal documents. Available on-line and on CD-ROM.

CIS/Index to Publications of the United States Congress. 1970–. Washington, DC: James B. Adler.

Indexes and abstracts all congressional publications, including committee hearings and reports, which are some of the most valuable government documents for American politics students.

U.S. Library of Congress. 1910–. *Monthly Checklist of State Publications*. Washington, DC: Government Printing Office.

Indexes the 10,000 state publications issued each year.

Your library will have a particularly full collection of government documents if it is one of the many official depositories of U.S. Government Publications. Ask your reference librarian if your library is a depository, where the collection is housed, and who the documents librarian is.

Other frequently overlooked sources of research material are legal publications, book reviews, newspapers, vertical files, public opinion surveys, handbooks, yearbooks, and almanacs.

Legal Publications

In every American government textbook is a chapter on the judiciary, which inevitably will refer to several landmark Supreme Court cases. The author also may mention a score of decisions of the Court in chapters on the Constitution, Congress, the Presidency, the Bureaucracy, and Civil Rights and Civil Liberties. Because the Supreme Court is an appellate court, it must give reasons justifying its exercises of power. These opinions of the Court, frequently accompanied by concurring and dissenting opinions written by justices who do not agree with the reasoning of the majority, can provide excellent foundations for class debates, essay examinations, and research papers. Most research papers, even the simplest, written in the introductory American government course could be enlivened and enriched by use of Supreme Court opinions (Lutzker 1988). Obvious topics such as abortion, gun control, school prayer, and pornography, as well as less "constitutional" issues like antitrust legislation and pollution, take on new dimensions when students go to court cases instead of relying simply on magazines and newspapers. These opinions can be found among the U.S. government documents under the title

United States Reports. 1754–. Washington, DC: Government Printing Office.

Supreme Court decisions are also available to depository libraries on-line. They are entered into the system the moment the Court announces its decision from the bench in Washington. You can read the syllabus of the decision and the justices' various opinions from the computer screen, print them, or download them onto your personal 3 1/2" or 5 1/4" disk. Supreme Court opinions are also published by private companies, including

Supreme Court Reporter. 1882–. St. Paul, MN: West.

United States Supreme Court Reports: Lawyers' Edition. 1956–. 2nd series. Rochester, NY: Lawyers' Co-op.

In order to find cases relevant to your topic, you should consult a legal digest. The digest functions as a subject index to the Supreme Court reports. Two easy-to-use digests are

U.S. Supreme Court Reports Digest: Lawyers' Edition. 1969–. Rochester, NY: Lawyers' Co-op.

U.S. Supreme Court Digest. 1944–. St. Paul, MN: West.

Another source for locating Supreme Court decisions by subject headings is

Reference Guide to the United States Supreme Court. 1986. New York: Facts on File.

Some of the legal concepts and terminology will be unfamiliar to you. Look them up in a legal dictionary or encyclopedia. The standard dictionary is

Black, H. C., et al. 1990. *Black's Law Dictionary.* 6th ed. St. Paul: West.

Encyclopedias also can be used to narrow your topic. For undergraduate American government students the best are

American Jurisprudence. 1962–. 2d ed. Rochester, NY: Lawyers' Co-op.

Guide to American Law: Everyone's Legal Encyclopedia. 1983–85. 12 vol. St. Paul, MN: West.

Similar to political science journals, law reviews publish scholarly articles on legal topics, usually written by law professors. The three best sources of law review articles relevant to American government topics in areas such as civil rights and civil liberties and the separation of powers are *ABC Pol Sci* (see above) and

Index to Legal Periodicals. 1909–. New York: Wilson.

Published monthly.

Current Law Index. 1980–. Foster City, CA: Information Access Co.

Reviews over 750 law reviews. Also available on microfilm and on-line computer databases such as *Legal Resources Index.*

A valuable use of these indexes is to trace the impact of an important court decision. For instance, in *INS* v. *Chadha* (1983), the Supreme Court invalidated the legislative veto, employed by Congress in hundreds of statutes to control executive branch agencies. If you wanted to know how significant the *Chadha* decision has been, you would consult the case citation appendix of a recent issue of the *Index to Legal Periodicals*. Under the case heading *INS* v. *Chadha* you would find references to numerous law review articles focusing on the case and its subsequent impact.

Student writers can extract even more value from Supreme Court decisions by reading the briefs, or arguments, submitted to the Court by the lawyers for the parties to the litigation. You can find this material in

Landmark Briefs and Arguments of the Supreme Court of the United States. 1978–. Frederick, MD: University Publications of America.

Book Reviews

A review written by a scholar in the field can save you the trouble of reading the book itself, for it can tell you whether that particular volume is relevant to your research. The reviewer may also give you insight into your topic and suggest other readings. Moreover, evaluation of books is necessary because they vary widely in quality. The single best source of book reviews in American politics is political science journals, most of which reserve substantial space for book reviews. A recently published book is often reviewed in several journals. You can locate the reviews of a particular book by consulting the book review section of the following indexes:

Social Sciences Index and *America: History and Life*.

A valuable periodical that reviews within sixty days of their publication books useful in American government research is

Perspective: Monthly Review of New Books in Government, Politics and International Affairs. 1972–. Washington, DC: Helen Dwight Reed Educational Foundation.

Another rich source is

Book Review Digest. 1906–. Bronx, NY: H. W. Wilson.

Contains excerpts from book reviews.

Newspapers

When conducting research on current issues, such as the confirmation battle over a presidential nomination to the Supreme Court or Congress's objection to a presidential decision in foreign policy, students find the following newspapers especially good sources of information on national events: the *New York Times,* the *Wall Street Journal,* the *Washington Post,* the *Los Angeles Times,* and the *Christian Science Monitor.* Each of these papers is indexed in

The National Newspaper Index. 1979–. Foster City, CA: Information Access Co.

Is available only on microfilm.

Some newspapers have their own index:

The New York Times Index. 1913–. New York: The New York Times.

Provides abstracts of each article.

The Wall Street Journal Index. 1958–. New York: Dow Jones & Co.

Provides abstracts of each article.

Washington Post Index. 1972–. Worster, Ohio: Newspaper Indexing Center.

Presents headlines only, no abstracts.

Vertical File

Libraries are unable to catalog the hundreds of booklets and pamphlets they receive each year. Much of this material is of only temporary interest anyway. Libraries, however, generally do make them available to patrons in a separate file called the vertical file. This can be a particularly useful resource in an American politics course, because it contains files on many political topics of current interest. Ask the reference librarian where the vertical file is located.

Sources of Facts and Statistics: Handbooks, Yearbooks, and Almanacs When there are two or more sides to a public policy or institutional reform issue, some of the best evidence to support your particular thesis will consist of statistics and other kinds of data. There are a number of sources of such information. Handbooks provide factual information, including statistics. Some particularly useful ones in American politics are

Book of the States. 1935–. Lexington, KY: Council of State Government.

Appears in a new edition every two years. Provides factual and statistical information about the governments of each of the fifty states. Is useful for topics involving state and local government.

U.S. Bureau of the Census. 1879–. *County and City Data Book.* Washington, DC: Government Printing Office.

Contains statistics concerning the economy and population of all U.S. cities and counties. Is updated every four years.

Municipal Year Book. 1933–. Washington, DC: International City Management Association.

Is published annually. Collects articles, statistical tables, lists, and graphs relating to city governments in the United States.

Scammon, R. M., ed. 1966–. *America Votes: A Handbook of Contemporary American Election Statistics.* Washington, DC: Congressional Quarterly.

Compiles voting statistics covering all national elections since 1954. Breaks down the vote by states and counties. Is useful for understanding the role of popular elections in explaining presidential and congressional behavior and is updated biennially.

Statistical Abstract of the United States. 1878–. Washington, DC: Government Printing Office.

Is considered the most reliable source of statistics on American economy, society, and politics. The subject index is a convenient guide to specific statistical tables.

Stanley, Harold W., and Richard G. Niemi. 1988. *Vital Statistics on American Politics.* Washington, DC: Congressional Quarterly.

Collects statistical tables, lists, and graphs relating to political topics such as abortion, gun control, campaigns, and elections.

Almanacs seek to cover more subject areas than handbooks, but in less depth. The general almanac most frequently consulted by students of American politics is

World Almanac. 1868–. New York: Newspaper Enterprise Association.

For a readable account of congressional and political activity, including major legislation, arranged in subject format, see

Congressional Quarterly Almanac. 1948–. Washington, DC: Congressional Quarterly.

Public opinion poll data are helpful to students who wish to document public support for or opposition to a particular policy or who wish to test an empirical hypothesis. To find the Gallup Poll most relevant to your topic, see the following monthly publication:

Gallup Opinion Index. 1965–. Princeton, NJ: Gallup International.

Example of a Search

Suppose your American government syllabus says, "Write a 5,000-word research paper on a topic in American politics." The paper is due in eight weeks—time to get started. The first step is to draw up a time estimate to manage the project. First divide the search into its specific steps and then calculate how long each task will take. Figure 5 shows what your completed estimate looks like.

Search Time Estimate

½ hr. Pick a topic.
¼ hr. Draft a working hypothesis.
¼ hr. Make a list of keywords.
¼ hr. Make a list of subject headings.
½ hr. Search the library catalog.
2 hrs. Skim books found. Take notes.
½ hr. Search periodicals indexes and abstracts.
1 hr. Skim articles found. Take notes.
½ hr. Search newspaper indexes.
1 hr. Skim stories found. Take notes
¾ hr. Search government documents indexes and abstracts.
1 hr. Skim documents and publications found.
½ hr. Test hypothesis in light of sources read. Modify if necessary.

9 hrs TOTAL

Figure 5 Search Time Estimate

Next, you schedule the nine hours needed to complete the search.

1. No subject pops into your mind, so you pick up your journal. While flipping the pages, you come across the entry you made on the textbook's discussion of the "iron triangle" thesis, according to which executive agencies (and their corresponding congressional committees) are often "captured" by the interests they were designed by Congress to regulate in the public interest. You recall that an example supportive of the thesis is the Department of Veterans Affairs, which would not dream of alienating the country's well-organized veterans organizations, and whose positions in support of the organizations' demands are supported by the House and Senate committees on veterans affairs. You note in your entry that the author says that iron triangles are more difficult to find now than in the past. One example cited is the Federal Communications Commission, originally founded by Congress to promote radio broadcasting but now facing competing pressures from both broadcasters and cable-television companies (Wilson 1992, 382). You wonder whether this competition has freed the FCC to regulate in the public interest. In other words, can you use it as an example of an "uncaptured" agency?

2. Your working hypothesis is that, because of conflicts among the various modes of delivering television signals, the FCC has been freed to regulate television in a way that advances the public good. In your search for materials, you follow these additional steps.

3. You make a list of keywords: Federal Communications Commission, cable television, television.

4. You consult the *Library of Congress Subject Headings* and look under "cable television." You find that "Cable Television—Law and Legislation" is the recommended heading.

5. Using this subject heading, you do a search on the library online catalog. Two books with identical titles, *Deregulation of Cable Television* with 1977 and 1980 publication dates, catch

your attention. You recall that the textbook implied that the FCC pursued a discriminatory policy against cable television and in favor of radio and television broadcasting. Deregulation, then, must mean freedom from this discriminatory policy. The books confirm the allegation of long-standing FCC favoritism toward the broadcast industry. But did this end? If so, when?

6. To get more current information, you decide to employ a periodicals abstract. Beginning with the most recent edition of *International Political Science Abstracts,* you look in the subject index under the headings "Cable television" and "Television." You find no entries until volume 40, no. 4–5, 1990. There you find in the subject index: "television—deregulation: 3803." You turn to abstract #3803, shown in Figure 6. So, the FCC *did* deregulate cable TV in the 1980s, and as a result it has become so competitive that the broadcasters of free television are demanding that it be reregulated! The article was published in 1989.

7. To find out if the FCC has returned to its earlier policy, as the author demands, you go to a newspaper index. The *Washing-*

40.3803 FERRALL, Victor E., Jr. — **The impact of television deregulation on private and public [US] interests.** *Journal of Communication* 39 (1), Winter 89 : 8-38.

A review of deregulatory actions by the US Federal Communications Commission during the 1980s shows that they had the effects of (1) increasing new entry into the commercial television market, particularly by entities with little or no prior experience and with inadequate financing, and (2) increasing the supply of commercial time available for sale. These effects, in turn, have resulted in a significant decline in the profitability of television stations, a decline which is continuing. The results of deregulation, coupled with growing competition to television stations from expanding new video distribution technologies, particularly cable, have materially curtailed public service programming offered by stations, and the diversity of their program offerings. These factors threaten the material degradation, and perhaps extinction, of local, free television, which the US has enjoyed for nearly half a century. Averting this outcome — if it can be averted — will require significant reregulation. [A]

Figure 6 Abstract #3803 (*International Political Science Abstracts.* 1990. 40:410.)

ton Post Index points you to an article published on May 15, 1991, which reports that a Senate committee the day before approved legislation to reregulate cable television. The report also says that the FCC will consider new cable regulations at its June meeting. What is still unclear, however, is when precisely cable was deregulated.

8. You go to the government documents department of the library and explain to the librarian on duty what you are looking for. The librarian recommends that you look in the index of *Major Studies and Issue Briefs of the Congressional Research Service, 1916–1989*. There, under the subject heading "cable television," you find an abstract of a 1984 Congressional Research Service report by Angele A. Gilroy entitled "Cable Television: Formation of a National Regulatory Policy." The abstract refers to the Cable Communications Policy Act of 1984. Was this the legislation that deregulated cable TV? Did the FCC oppose or support deregulation? You ask how can you learn more about this particular act.

9. The librarian refers you to

Congress and the Nation: A Review of Government and Politics, Vol. 6, 1981–1984. 1985. Washington, DC: Congressional Quarterly.

In the index, you find "Cable TV—deregulation: 279–281." There you find an essay on the background of the 1984 act, which indicates that the cable television industry began to boom in the 1970s as a result of FCC relaxation of its controls. As FCC regulation decreased, however, local governments increased their control. The 1984 act's main purpose was to free cable from local government rate setting and regulation. The question remains what triggered the FCC's deregulatory course in the late 1970s and early 1980s.

10. You return to the general reference department. It is clear that reregulation of cable television is a topic of current interest, so you go to Congressional Quarterly's *Editorial Research Reports,* a weekly publication focusing on a different political controversy each week. In the 1980–1990 cumulative index, you find

under the subject heading "cable television" that the December 7, 1990, issue was devoted to the question, "Does Cable TV Need More Regulation?" In the introduction to this issue, you learn that since the late 1970s the following industries have been competing in the television signal delivery business: broadcast television, cable television, direct-broadcast satellite systems, satellite master antenna television, wireless cable, and telephone companies.

You still have a lot of research to do, both in the reference and government documents departments, but what you have found so far seems to confirm your hypothesis that conflict among competing interest groups weakened broadcast television's influence over the FCC, permitting it to regulate the television signal delivery industry with a view toward the public interest. This finding, if it holds up, further calls into question the iron triangle thesis. Figure 7 shows an activity schematic for a typical search.

If you significantly modify your hypothesis, you may need to repeat the search process. Sources not mentioned, such as almanacs and handbooks, can be added or substituted for the search aids listed. Adjust your search to the nature of the topic and the extent of your own existing knowledge on the subject.

Documenting Sources

As the writer of a research paper, one of the important decisions you must make is how to document sources. Your instructor may require a particular method or may leave that choice up to you. What is essential is that, whichever format you use, you are consistent and accurate in its application. Some of the most common style guides are Turabian (1987), MLA (Modern Language Association) (1988), the *Chicago Manual of Style* (1982), APA (American Psychological Association) (1983), and the *Style Manual for Political Science* (1988), a publication of the American Political Science Association's (APSA's) Committee on Publications. Because of its wide acceptance among political scientists, including usage in the discipline's premier journal, the *American Political Science Review,* I have chosen to present the APSA format. Below are examples of

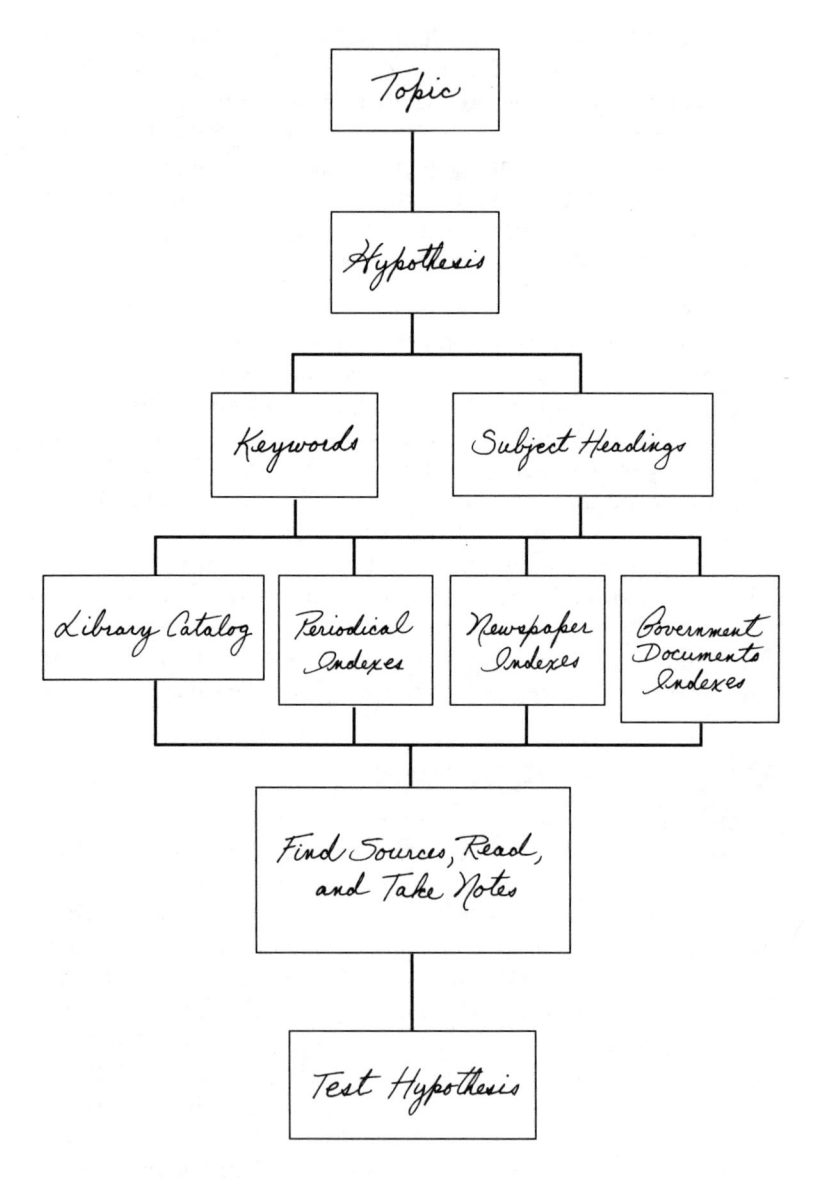

Figure 7 Search Activity Schematic

only the most common types of citations and references. If you don't find an answer to your question here, consult the *Style Manual for Political Science* or the *Chicago Manual of Style*, copies of which should be in your library's reference section.

Under the APSA system, footnotes or endnotes are hardly used. Include a note only if you must add essential information that supplements, but cannot be integrated into, the text of your paper. Notes should be numbered consecutively throughout the paper. Use raised arabic numerals (like this[1]) to call attention to a note. Type all notes on a separate sheet, headed "Notes," and place the sheet between the end of the text and the References.

Citations

When using the words, data, or ideas of another writer, you credit the source by means of a parenthetical citation. This enables the reader to locate the source in the list of references at the end of your essay. Insert the author's last name and the year of publication parenthetically in the text. Include the page number as well if you have used a paraphrase or summary of a passage or a direct quotation (do not use the abbreviations *p.* or *pp.*).

> According to a recent study of direct democracy (Cronin 1989)...

If the author's name or the date (or both) are mentioned in the text, they should be omitted from the parenthetical information.

> A 1989 study of direct democracy (Cronin) shows...

> Cronin's study of direct democracy (1989) shows...

> In 1989 Cronin demonstrated...

- *Work by Two Authors*

Cite both names each time the reference occurs.

> A study of environmental administration found that it is not nature that needs managing but rather "people's behavior relative to natural resources" (Henning and Mangun 1989, 6). [The page number refers to the location of the quotation.]

- *Work by More Than Two and Fewer Than Six Authors*
  Cite all names in the first reference; after that, use only the surname of the first author followed by *et al.* (Latin for "and others").

  (Abramson, Arterton, and Orren 1988) [first citation]

  (Abramson et al. 1988) [subsequent citations]

- *Work by Six or More Authors*
  Cite the surname of the first author followed by *et al.*

  This was disputed by Lopach et al. (1990)

- *Work by an Institutional Author*
  Authorship of a work is sometimes attributed to a society, a government agency, or some other institution. In this case, the institution is cited as the author.

  (American Political Science Association 1991)

  Common abbreviations may be used or an abbreviation established in the first citation to be used subsequently, provided the meaning is clear.

  (AFL-CIO 1990) [common abbreviation]

  (American Federation of Teachers [AFT] 1989) [first citation]

  (AFT 1989) [subsequent citations]

- *Work with No Author Given*
  When a book or article appears without an author's name, use the title instead. Pamphlets, magazine and newspaper articles, and even books may lack a byline.

  ("President Demands Line-Item Veto" 1991)

- *Entire Issue of a Journal*

  ("Housing Policy" 1991)

- *Two or More Works within Parentheses*

Works by the same author(s) are arranged in order of publication.

(Abramowitz 1985, 1986)

Works by different authors are arranged alphabetically by surnames.

Several studies have reached the same conclusion (Brown 1984; Jacobson and Kernell 1978; Stanley 1988).

- *Personal Communication (letters, interviews, telephone conversations)*

    (Senator Albert Gore, personal communication, 17 July 1990)

Personal communications are not included in the list of references because they cannot be consulted by the reader.

- *Government Documents*

    (U.S. Internal Revenue Service 1991)

- *Government Hearings*

    (Sussman 1984)

- *Court Cases*

    (*Roe* v. *Wade* 1973)

- *Statutes*

    (Federal Salary Act of 1967)

Consult *A Uniform System of Citation* (1981) for more details on how to cite court cases and statutes.

References

The list of references at the end of an article or paper identifies the sources used and cited by the author, enabling the reader to retrieve them. It includes every reference cited in the paper and no other. It is not a bibliography, which is a comprehensive catalog of all the works published on a particular topic. Although each part of a paper should be done with great care, compiling the list of references calls for exacting precision. A misspelled name, an incorrect page number, an omitted date—any of these will trouble the reader and call into question the accuracy of the research and the researcher.

The list of references begins on a separate page. The word *References* is centered at the top. The entries are listed alphabetically by the authors' last names or, in the case of institutional authorship, by the first significant word of the name. Use hanging indention: The first line of each entry begins at the left margin; subsequent lines are indented three spaces. You can save yourself much time if you have recorded the information in the correct format on a bibliography card. Mark each card bearing a title that you cite in the paper with a check in the upper right-hand corner, arrange the cards in alphabetical order, and simply copy them onto your paper.

References to Periodicals

- *Journal Article by One Author*

    DiStefano, Christine. 1986. "Dilemmas of Difference: Feminism, Modernity, and Postmodernism." *Women and Politics* 8:1–24. [8 is the volume number and is followed by the inclusive pages of the article.]

- *Journal Article by Two or More Authors*

    Greeno, Catherine G., and Eleanor E. Maccoby. 1986. "How Different Is the 'Different Voice'?" *Signs: Journal of Women in Culture and Society* 11:310–16.

- *Magazine Article*

    Howe, Irving. 1991. "The Value of the Canon." *New Republic*, 18 February, pp. 40–7.

- *Newspaper Article*

    Broder, David. 1986. "Reagan on the Campaign Trail: Right in Every Way." *New Orleans Times-Picayune,* 5 November.

- *Newspaper Article, No Author*

    "Agency Revises Rules on Asbestos to Stress Sealing Off of Mineral." 1985. *Wall Street Journal,* 7 August.

- *Book Review*

    Atwood, Barbara. 1991. *Review of Silent Revolution: The Transformation of Divorce Law in the United States* by Herbert Jacob. In *American Political Science Review* 85:289–91.

References to Books

- *Book by One Author*

    Lockhart, Charles. 1989. *Gaining Ground: Tailoring Social Programs to American Values.* Berkeley: University of California Press.

- *Book by Two or More Authors*

    Bardach, Eugene, and Robert A. Kagan. 1982. *Going by the Book: The Problem of Regulatory Unreasonableness.* Philadelphia: Temple University Press.

- *Book by an Institutional Author*

    U.S. General Accounting Office. 1979. *How Effective Are OSHA's Complaint Procedures?* Washington, D.C.: Government Printing Office.

- *Chapter in a Book*

    Moe, Terry M. 1989. "The Politics of Bureaucratic Structure." In *Can Government Govern?* eds. John Chubb and Paul Peterson. Washington, D.C.: Brookings.

- *Edited Book*

    Harmel, Robert, ed. 1984. *Presidents and Their Parties*. New York: Praeger.

- *Report*

    Centaur Associates. 1985. *The Impact of OSHA Enforcement Activities*. Report to the Occupational Safety and Health Administration.

- *Governmental Hearing*

    Posner, Paul L. 1990. *Testimony in Collecting Unpaid Taxes: Why Can't the IRS Do Better?* Hearing Before the Committee on Governmental Affairs. Senate, 1 August, pp. 13–26.

- *Court Case*

    Roe v. *Wade*. 1973. 410 U.S. 113.

- *Statute*

    Federal Salary Act of 1967. 1976. 2 U.S.C. 356.

- Unpublished Paper Presented at a Meeting

    Ayres, Ian, and John Braithwaite. 1989. "Tri-partism, Empowerment, and Game-theoretic Notions of Regulatory Capture." Presented to the Law and Society Association Meeting, Madison, Wisconsin.

Appendix: Careers in Political Science

Many students find their first political science course so fascinating and engaging that they choose to take additional courses and to major or minor in the discipline. What are the career options open to holders of the baccalaureate degree in political science? There are in fact a variety of professional careers open to political science majors.

Business

Many graduates are hired by the same business firms that employ majors in the other liberal arts, such as history, philosophy, or English. Political science majors have chosen careers in finance, banking, public relations, advertising, human resource management, and marketing. A number of majors will go immediately upon graduation into a management trainee position. Many employers are impressed by the knowledge political science students have of the relationship between business and government and by their writing and analytical skills. Those who do not pursue business careers tend to pursue futures in law, government, journalism, lobbying, or teaching.

Law

Although many prelaw students major in political science, law schools, unlike medical schools, require no particular undergraduate course of study. Law schools admit applicants from a wide variety of academic backgrounds. Admissions officers and committees base their decisions largely on the applicant's undergraduate grade point average and score on the Law School Admissions Test (LSAT). Political science courses emphasizing writing and analytical thinking will prepare you best for the LSAT and for legal studies.

Government

The political science major may find a position in nearly any agency or branch of the federal government. The federal government, in fact, is this country's largest single employer. Many political science majors are interested in careers with the foreign service, the United States' diplomatic, consular, commercial, and overseas cultural and information service. It assists the President and Secretary of State in planning, conducting, and implementing our foreign policy. Successful applicants must pass both a written examination and an oral interview. Employment with all federal agencies, however, is very competitive. There has been little growth in the number of civilian federal employees over the past twenty years.

By contrast, there has been significant growth in the number of state and local government employees, and political science majors may find substantial opportunities there. The federal government is turning more and more responsibility for the administration of federally funded programs over to state and local agencies. A popular choice with political science majors is working in the electoral campaign of a political candidate—an experience that may result in government employment.

Interest Groups

There are hundreds of public and private groups that attempt to influence in an organized way government decision makers. Contrary to popular perceptions, the greatest source of the influence of pressure groups is not money or other material rewards offered to legislators but information. The organizations with the greatest at stake in a policy change have the greatest incentive to conduct research so as to calculate accurately how it would affect them. The data they gather is often the best (or all) that is available to an administrator or lawmaker. Although some private trade associations hire lobbyists from within their ranks, others prefer to recruit persons from outside the group who understand the political system and possess skills of effective oral and written communication. There is an especially keen demand for recent college graduates among groups such as Common Cause that aspire to represent the public interest. Employment opportunities with such organizations are pretty well confined to Washington and the state capitals (Curzan 1981).

Journalism

Some of the best known journalists, such as Bob Woodward of the *Washington Post* and Anthony Lewis of the *New York Times,* write on political topics. Typically, 50 percent of a national newspaper's front page is devoted to political news. Political science, thus, is a logical major for those interested in a career in the print and electronic media. Writing skills, of course, are critical, as well as knowledge of local, state, and national politics.

Teaching

Junior and senior high schools, in general, do not offer courses in political science. Nevertheless, some state boards of education do require all high school students to take one or two semesters of American government. Political science majors interested in a teaching career at the secondary level should also have a strong preparation in American or world history (Curzan 1981). Coursework in geography and sociology will also be useful to the "social studies" teacher. Some states require all teachers to have completed a certain number of education credits at the collegiate level to be eligible for certification, whereas others are more flexible. Most teaching opportunities for political science majors are at the junior college, college, and university level. The first requires a master's degree, and the last two typically a doctorate.

For more information on any of these career opportunities, visit your college's office of career guidance and placement.

No matter what your eventual career choice is, as an adult you have a variety of responsibilities and rights as a partner in the

American experiment in self-government. Legally enforceable public duties include payment of income taxes, service as a juror in civil and criminal trials, and, for men, registration for possible military conscription. Although there is no penalty for failing to do so, as there is in some countries, we are also expected to register to vote and to cast ballots during elections for local, state, and federal offices. All citizens, regardless of race, gender, or social class, are free to express their views in public on matters of public importance, to associate with others who share their views, and to run for elected office. Surveys show that citizens' satisfaction with their political system is closely related to their own sense of efficacy. The more you know about the theory and practice of liberal democracy in the United States, the more effective you will be as an informed voter, taxpayer, and consumer of government services.

References

Adler, Mortimer J., and Charles Van Doren. 1972. *How to Read a Book*. New York: Simon and Schuster.

Biddle, Arthur W., and John H. Clarke, eds. 1991. *The Thinking Book: Critical Thinking Across the Curriculum*. Englewood Cliffs, NJ: Prentice-Hall.

Chicago Manual of Style. 1982. 13th ed. Chicago: University of Chicago Press.

Cohen, Jeffrey E., Michael A. Krassa, and John A. Hamman. 1991. "The Impact of Presidential Campaigning on Midterm U.S. Senate Elections." *American Political Science Review* 85: 165–78.

Curzan, Mary H., ed. 1981. *Careers and the Study of Political Science: A Guide for Undergraduates*. 3d ed. Washington, DC: American Political Science Association.

Fulwiler, Toby. 1987. "Keeping a Journal." In *Writer's Guide: Political Science*, eds. Arthur W. Biddle and Kenneth M. Holland. Lexington, MA: D. C. Heath.

Lunsford, Andrea, and Robert Connors. 1989. *The St. Martin's Handbook*. New York: St. Martin's Press.

Lutzker, Marilyn. 1988. *Research Projects for College Students: What to Write Across the Curriculum*. New York: Greenwood Press.

MLA Handbook for Writers of Research Papers. 1988. 3d ed. New York: Modern Language Association.

Nist, Sherrie L., and William Diehl. 1990. *Developing Textbook Thinking*. 2d ed. Lexington, MA: D. C. Heath.

Publication Manual of the American Psychological Association. 1983. 3d ed. Washington, DC: American Psychological Association.

Rudolph, Janell, and Rebecca Argall. 1990. *Resources and Research in the MSU Libraries*. Dubuque, IA: Kendall/Hunt Publishing.

Style Manual for Political Science. 1988. Washington, DC: American Political Science Association.

Turabian, Kate L. 1987. *A Manual for Writers of Term Papers, Theses, and Dissertations*. 5th ed. Chicago: University of Chicago Press.

Uniform System of Citation. 1981. 13th ed. Cambridge, MA: The Harvard Law Review Association.

Wilson, James Q. 1992. *American Government: Institutions and Policies.* 5th ed. Lexington, MA: D. C. Heath.

Ziegler, Zig. 1988. *Goals.* Chicago: Nightingale-Conant.

Leslie M. Jumper